Populism,
Its Rise and Fall

Populism,
Its Rise and Fall

William A. Peffer

Edited and with an Introduction by
Peter H. Argersinger

 University Press of Kansas

© 1992 by the University Press of Kansas
All rights reserved
Photographs courtesy of Kansas State Historical Society

Published by the University Press of Kansas (Lawrence, Kansas
66049), which was organized by the Kansas Board of Regents and is
operated and funded by Emporia State University, Fort Hays State
University, Kansas State University, Pittsburg State University,
the University of Kansas, and Wichita State University

Library of Congress Cataloging-in-Publication Data

Peffer, William Alfred, 1831–1912.
    Populism, its rise and fall / William A. Peffer : edited with an
introduction by Peter H. Argersinger.
        p.   cm.
    Includes bibliographical references and index.
    ISBN 0-7006-0509-6 (alk. paper)
    1. People's Party of the United States—History—19th century—
Sources.   2. Populism—United States—History—19th century—
Sources.   3. Populism—Kansas—History—19th century—
Sources.
    I. Argersinger, Peter H.   II. Title.
    JK2372.P44   1991
    324.2732—dc20   91-18795
                                                        CIP

British Library Cataloguing in Publication Data is available.

Printed in the United States of America
10 9 8 7 6 5 4 3 2 1

Contents

Editor's Preface

William A. Peffer's *Populism: Its Rise and Fall* was first published as a series of essays in the *Chicago Tribune* in 1899. In its re-
publication in this volume I have made only a few minor changes in
the original text. I have corrected obvious typographical errors in
spelling or punctuation, and I have revised several features obviously introduced by the *Tribune* in its effort to make the work con-
form to the contemporary practices or requirements of newspaper
publication. With few exceptions, for instance, I have removed the
subheads that the *Tribune* inserted; similarly, I have reformatted
statistical tables that the *Tribune* awkwardly altered to fit the space
limitations of newspaper columns. All notes and bracketed words
are my editorial additions, as are the titles for the first two chapters,
which were originally untitled.

Senator Peffer did the crucial work for this volume, but several
other people also made important contributions that should be acknowledged. Jo Ann E. Argersinger generously provided encour-
agement, assistance, and valuable advice in preparing this edition.
For help in transcribing, typing, and other essential tasks, I am indebted to Rochelle Sandbank, Rachael D. Schene, and especially
Linda M. Hatmaker. I also am indebted to Cynthia Miller of the
University Press of Kansas. Her interest and support made this volume possible and ensured that an important perspective on Populism was once again available.

Editor's Introduction

In early spring 1890, the *Atchison Globe* reacted to rumors that the discontented farmers of Kansas were organizing politically and intended to elect William A. Peffer to the United States Senate in place of the veteran Republican John J. Ingalls. "Who in the hello is Peffer?" it indignantly queried. Little more than a year later, the *Washington Post* described Peffer as "the most extensively advertised Senator that ever came to Washington." In the short interval between those two very different editorial comments, a remarkable development had obviously occurred. Because of Peffer's central importance, some contemporary observers initially described that development as Pefferism; eventually it became known as Populism.[1]

The *Globe*'s editor had revealed his own ignorance more than he had indicated Peffer's standing in dismissing him so contemptuously. Peffer had already played a significant political role in Kansas for some time by 1890, first as a Republican state legislator in the 1870s and a presidential elector in 1880, and then, more importantly, as an editor for several Topeka daily newspapers and the *Kansas Farmer*, the state's leading agricultural journal and its most widely circulated newspaper. In this last position, Peffer used his

---

1. *Atchison Globe* quoted in *Lawrence Daily Journal*, March 16, 1890; *Washington Post*, December 8, 1891.

considerable influence throughout the 1880s to encourage farmers to organize and promote their own interests by seeking political and economic reforms. But the *Globe*'s editor was correct in thinking that Peffer was scarcely a prominent politician, or one likely to challenge the traditional Republican domination of Kansas politics, of which Ingalls's lengthy senatorial career was symbolic.[2] But when the state's farmers, engulfed by economic distress and rebuffed by indifferent political institutions, at last followed Peffer's advice, first organizing into the Farmers' Alliance and then creating their own political party—the People's or Populist party—Peffer naturally emerged as the movement's most conspicuous figure.

After helping engineer an astonishing Populist victory in the most tumultuous campaign in Kansas history in 1890, Peffer was elected as the first Populist United States Senator in a contest that attracted intense national attention. He then campaigned actively to spread the Kansas contagion among farmers throughout the West and South and helped organize the national People's party, chairing the 1891 reform convention in Cincinnati that launched the new party. "I have a sort of fatherly interest in the People's Party," he later recalled to a group of Iowa Populists. "I am in some measure responsible for its existence. I had the honor of presiding over the conference that begat it, and I witnessed the travail of its birth." Thereafter Peffer continued to play a prominent national role in the party. He helped plan its political strategy and was frequently mentioned as a possible Populist presidential candidate; he worked determinedly to advance the party's principles of economic and political reform, both in drafting legislation in the Senate and in publicizing these principles through his voluminous writ-

2. For an account of the *Globe*'s editor, a misanthropic conservative whose epigrams brought him national recognition and who always promoted the political career of his fellow Atchison resident, John J. Ingalls, see Calder M. Pickett, *Ed Howe: Country Town Philosopher* (Lawrence: University Press of Kansas, 1968). For Ingalls himself, see the sympathetic biography by Burton J. Williams, *Senator John James Ingalls: Kansas' Iridescent Republican* (Lawrence: University Press of Kansas, 1972).

ings and frequent speeches; and he vigorously promoted the party's organizational and campaign activities, especially by editing the most important Populist newspaper, the Topeka *Advocate*, by establishing and subsidizing other party newspapers, including the *National Watchman*, and by serving as the president of the National Reform Press Association, a crusading organization of Populist editors. It was this prominence as ideologue, publicist, and politician that was reflected in the early common use of such phrases as "Pefferism" for Populism and "Pefferites" or "Peffercrats" for Populists.[3]

Peffer came to personify Populism in another way as well. Political cartoonists seized upon his distinctive physical appearance—tall and thin, dressed in black, wearing boots and hat but no collar or tie, above all with a beard reaching nearly to his waist—and consistently employed it in caricature to symbolize the People's party. The bewhiskered image of Peffer, as the historian Roger A. Fischer has written, served as "the ubiquitous symbol of the Populist presence in American politics."[4]

But neither Populism nor the People's party was ever altogether a united, coherent entity, certainly not one fully embodied by Peffer, however important he was or prototypical he appeared to be. Built largely upon the structure of the Farmers' Alliance, the People's party was created out of quarreling groups of disaffected Republicans, dissident Democrats, Greenbackers, Union Laborites, and Prohibitionists, united only by economic hardship and com-

3. Topeka *Advocate*, August 25, 1897; Peter H. Argersinger, *Populism and Politics: William Alfred Peffer and the People's Party* (Lexington: University Press of Kentucky, 1974), passim. For the remarkable circumstances that surrounded Peffer's election and brought him to national attention, see Peter H. Argersinger, "The Most Picturesque Drama: The Kansas Senatorial Election of 1891," *Kansas Historical Quarterly* 38 (Spring 1972): 43–64.

4. Roger A. Fischer, "Rustic Rasputin: William A. Peffer in Color Cartoon Art, 1891–1899," *Kansas History* 11 (Winter 1988–1989): 222–239, esp. 225.

mon opposition to the continued hegemony of the major parties, Republicans in the West, Democrats in the South. Peffer served (as one Populist newspaper later admitted) "very well for a figure-head when the party was new and its members comparative strangers to one another."[5] But as the party and its adherents gradually changed in response to the political and economic conditions of the decade, as they fashioned organizations and strategies to create successful political coalitions in different states, as they confronted entrenched political opponents and the institutionalized two-party system, the fault lines within the Populist party began to emerge.

Many Republicans who joined the new party carried with them their traditional hostility to Democrats—what one called "their hereditary foe." Dissatisfaction with Republican politicians and policies did not necessarily reduce their antipathies to Democratic personnel and programs. The famous Kansas Populist Mary E. Lease, for example, always retained what she called "an intense hatred" for Democrats and was never comfortable cooperating with them within the People's party even as she begged her listeners, "Forget party affiliations of the past . . . in this great struggle for our homes."[6] Peffer himself held similar attitudes. An ardent Republican since the party's formation in 1854, he left it only reluctantly in 1890. He and his family had suffered greatly at the hands of Democrats in the past, he disliked their continuing opposition to an activ-

5. *LeRoy Reporter* quoted in Topeka *Advocate*, January 6, 1897.

6. Independence *Star & Kansan*, December 9, 1898; Katherine B. Clinton, "What Did You Say, Mrs. Lease?" *Kansas Quarterly* 1 (Fall 1969): 54n; *Fort Scott Daily Monitor*, August 14, 1890. For an argument that Lease was "psychologically incapable of cooperating with Democrats" because of her "deep resentment against the Democratic party," see O. Gene Clanton, "Intolerant Populist? The Disaffection of Mary Elizabeth Lease," *Kansas Historical Quarterly* 34 (Summer 1968): 195–196. Indeed, Lease soon returned to the GOP when she became convinced that politics had "resolved itself into the old issue of copperheadism versus Republicanism, and as the daughter of an old Union soldier I feel that my place is with the Republican party." Kansas Biographical Scrapbook, "L," vol. 1, p. 130, Kansas State Historical Society (KSHS), Topeka.

ist government and their hostility to prohibition, and he hoped to minimize their influence within the People's party.[7] However latent was the antagonism that Republican Populists felt toward former Democrats now allied with them in the People's party, any proposal that the new party pursue fusion with Democrats still committed to their old party provoked outrage. As one South Dakota Populist maintained, "We did not leave the corrupt Republican party to hobnob with the rotten Democratic party."[8]

For their part, Democrats who abandoned their party to help launch the People's party often retained a residual animosity toward the former Republicans with whom they now worked. Upholding traditional ideas and a local perspective, they favored free silver as "the dollar of our daddies" but were uneasy with what they perceived as the "paternalism" of the interventionist government proposed by their new colleagues or its threat to the hallowed concept of "personal liberty."[9] In the South, such apprehensive feelings were further complicated by bitter memories of the Civil War and by the established racial alignments in politics; in several states discontented Democrats demonstrated the difficulty of breaking with their hoary party by first naming their new organizations "Jeffersonian Democrats" before finally merging with the

7. For a discussion of an earlier violent episode that confirmed Peffer's distrust of Democrats, see Peter H. Argersinger, "The Conservative as Radical: A Reconstruction Dilemma," *Tennessee Historical Quarterly* 34 (Summer 1975): 168–187.

8. *Clear Lake Advocate* quoted in *Brookings County Press* (Brookings, S.Dak.), November 2, 1893.

9. For a valuable discussion of the persistence of traditional Democratic attitudes, see R. Hal Williams, " 'Dry Bones and Dead Language': The Democratic Party," in *The Gilded Age*, ed. H. Wayne Morgan (Syracuse, N.Y.: Syracuse University Press, 1970), 129–148. The limits even to the economic radicalism of some Democrats attracted to the Farmers' Alliance and Populism can be seen in William F. Holmes, "The Southern Farmers' Alliance and the Georgia Senatorial Election of 1890," *Journal of Southern History* 50 (May 1984): 197–224.

People's party.[10] Populist fusion schemes in the South involved cooperating with Republicans rather than with Democrats, as in the West, but still roused basic political hostilities. An Alabama Populist, for example, condemned efforts to have the third party "affiliate with Negroes, carpetbaggers, and Republicans," while a Tennesseean warned that fusion would "drive the Third Party back to the Democrats."[11] Indeed, the political sectionalism of the third party system complicated further the task of creating a third national party, for it required bringing together contrasting regional minorities, which in turn enabled the major parties to play upon sectional and partisan prejudices to prevent defections to the new party. As one Kansas Populist complained, "In the south, people are told that this movement is of northern origin, a Republican device to disrupt the Democratic party, strike down white rule, and establish black supremacy instead, while in the north, politicians tell us the movement is a southern institution, devised by southern Democrats . . . and designed to destroy the Republican

10. William Warren Rogers, *The One-Gallused Rebellion: Agrarianism in Alabama, 1865–1896* (Baton Rouge: Louisiana State University Press, 1970), 189, 209–213, 271–273, 290; Roscoe C. Martin, *The People's Party in Texas: A Study in Third Party Politics* (Austin: University of Texas Bulletin, 1933), 42–43. In Kansas in 1892, a Populist faction that opposed fusing with Democrats or nominating Democratic Populists but disdained a return to the GOP organized a comparable halfway house and called themselves the Abraham Lincoln Republicans. See Argersinger, *Populism and Politics*, 143, 179.

11. Quotations in Gerald H. Gaither, *Blacks and the Populist Revolt: Ballots and Bigotry in the "New South"* (University: University of Alabama Press, 1977), 69, and Roger L. Hart, *Redeemers, Bourbons, and Populists: Tennessee, 1870–1896* (Baton Rouge: Louisiana State University Press, 1975), 196. For a recent study that emphasizes that Southern fusion efforts were undermined by "the racial stigma attached to Republicanism" and resulted in white defections from among Democratic Populists, see Gregg Cantrell and D. Scott Barton, "Texas Populists and the Failure of Biracial Politics," *Journal of Southern History* 55 (November 1989): 659–692.

party of the north . . . and thereby abrogate all the results of the war."[12]

There were also tensions surrounding the Populist affiliations of former Greenbackers, Union Laborites, Socialists, Prohibitionists, and other members of previous third party efforts. Some Populists from the major parties regarded these veteran reformers as eccentric malcontents and feared that the party might become "an asylum for all the cranks in the universe." One party official even proposed purging these "cranks, anarchists, and socialists" who insisted upon greater reforms than simply free silver.[13] Populists of third-party antecedents naturally often had their own reservations about their new colleagues from the major parties, sometimes doubting the sincerity of these latecomers to reform politics. One reporter, for instance, described "the suspicion" held by former Union Laborites that some of their new allies in the People's party had "too much Republican blood in their veins to be up to the wild-and-wooly standard of reform."[14] Prohibitionists welcomed the support they found among Populists for their interests in electoral and monetary reforms but were appalled at the continuing hostility of former Democrats to their main objective itself. Populists of third-party antecedents, moreover, often brought with them conflicting conclusions from their previous political experiences. Some believed that political fusion with a major party had brought their earlier third party to ruin; others like James B. Weaver of Iowa saw in fusion their only hope for success.

These divisions within the People's party, then, involved not merely matters of partisan prejudice and emotionalism, but also important issues of basic political philosophy such as the role of the government, party positions with respect to social and eco-

12. Quoted in O. Gene Clanton, *Kansas Populism: Ideas and Men* (Lawrence: University Press of Kansas, 1969), 268.

13. Martin, *People's Party in Texas*, 88; P. W. Couzins to Henry Demarest Lloyd, December 30, 1894, Henry Demarest Lloyd Papers, State Historical Society of Wisconsin, Madison.

14. *Topeka Daily Capital*, January 24, 1891.

nomic reform, and immediate campaign tactics such as fusion. And these conflicts regularly appeared in the Populist efforts to cobble together platforms encompassing their differing objectives, the negotiations to nominate composite tickets reflecting the constituent elements in the party, the struggles for organizational control of the party, or the checkered performances of the party's legislators.[15]

Each of these areas of controversy produced some reshuffling of the Populist coalition. In 1892, for instance, fusion with Republicans in Georgia, North Carolina, and other Southern states drove many Democratic Populists back to their first party home, prompting a Virginia Democratic party official to claim that "the Third party is rapidly resolving itself back into the Democratic party from which it was mainly drawn."[16] Similarly, fusion with Democrats in Kansas, Minnesota, and other Western states drove some Republican Populists back to the GOP, one reporter describing their decision by paraphrasing their complaints with the statement that "they did not leave the Republican party to go body and soul over to the Democracy; that if it has to be one of the old parties they will return to the one they naturally belong to."[17]

Most Populists, however, accommodated themselves to the various compromises in platforms, candidates, and tactics in the hope of winning elections that would presumably place their party in a position to implement necessary reforms. And other recruits con-

15. For examples of each of these instances, see, respectively, Jack S. Blocker, Jr., "The Politics of Reform: Populists, Prohibition, and Woman Suffrage, 1891–1892," *Historian* 34 (August 1972): 614–632; Rogers, *One-Gallused Rebellion*, 295–300, 304–311; Lawrence Goodwyn, *Democratic Promise: The Populist Moment in America* (New York: Oxford University Press, 1976), 407–423; Peter H. Argersinger, "Populists in Power: Public Policy and Legislative Behavior," *Journal of Interdisciplinary History* 18 (Summer 1987): 81–105.

16. Quoted in William DuBose Sheldon, *Populism in the Old Dominion: Virginia Farm Politics, 1885–1900* (Princeton, N.J.: Princeton University Press, 1935), 88.

17. *Topeka Daily Capital*, July 20, 1892.

tinued to join the party, particularly after a lengthy and devastating depression began in 1893 and neither major party responded effectively to the national discontent. In the 1894 elections, Populists increased their national vote dramatically, and the growing popular interest in the free and unlimited coinage of silver seemed to augur even greater success, but disagreements over the proper course to pursue and contests for control of the party continued to trouble the Populists. The famous and climactic election of 1896, in which the Populists agreed to subordinate both their party and its distinctive principles by endorsing the Democratic presidential nomination of William Jennings Bryan, brought the party's internal tensions to a head. When the Bryan campaign failed, the People's party began to collapse as well.

Peffer personally experienced the party's fragmentation when he failed to win reelection to the Senate in 1897, despite Populist control of the Kansas legislature. Although universally regarded as "a faithful, tireless worker" for the original Populist principles, Peffer was condemned for his opposition to fusion and the political compromises its achievement demanded. His faction of former Republicans who opposed fusion and advocated comprehensive reform no longer controlled the party. "My defeat [he later observed] satisfied me that the politicians of the People's party in Kansas did not want a Senator that was not acceptable to the Democratic party." Indeed, in order to ensure subsequent fusion and placate Democratic demands for recognition, the Populist legislators elected Peffer's polar opposite in the party: William A. Harris, a former Democrat—indeed a former Confederate soldier, the state's foremost fusionist, and a conservative whose commitment to reform was so limited that he not only opposed such distinctive Populist demands as the subtreasury and debtor relief but was even prepared to accept a revision in the coinage ratio for silver, a position abhorred by inflationists. Democrats delightedly hailed Harris as one of their own, prompting speculation that Harris would caucus with the Democrats rather than the Populists in the Senate. One disconsolate Populist legislator observed that Harris had always "consorted with Democrats" and only "pretended to be a friend of the Populist cause."[18]

In Kansas state politics, the fragmentation and collapse of the People's party was illustrated in the disspirited performance of the Populists in the 1897 legislature, where despite their control they engaged in endless wrangling and failed to enact legislation to fulfill their platform pledges. With the lobbying assistance of Jerry Simpson, another Populist seeking Democratic approval, Harris sidetracked the promised reform measures, and soon the legislature dissolved into a divided and contentious body with commonplace allegations of bribery and betrayal. It finally adjourned thoroughly discredited, with one Populist editor convinced that the party had suffered "a more ignominious defeat, than if our candidates had failed of election." Efforts by Populist Governor John Leedy to hold the collapsing fusion coalition together by dispensing patronage to Democrats and refusing to enforce prohibition simply further divided the party.[19]

Nationally, the party appeared even more hopeless and disrupted. The 1896 campaign had been a disaster in the South especially. Some Populists, like Reuben Kolb of Alabama, welcomed the Bryanized Democracy and returned to their old party. Other Populists, like Kolb's Alabama associate Warren Reese, so feared incorporation into the Democratic party, which had violently attacked them, that they actually joined the GOP in reaction. Others were torn in both directions when the People's party fused with the Republicans on state tickets and Democrats on the national ticket. While Marion Butler, the chair of the Populist National Committee, defended such policies as pragmatic, others saw them as sui-

18. Topeka *Advocate*, December 16, 1896; Kansas Biographical Scrapbook, vol. 137, pp. 97–98, KSHS; *Kansas Semi-Weekly Capital* (Topeka), October 12, March 9, 1897; Argersinger, *Populism and Politics*, 276–281.
    19. *Norton Liberator*, March 12, 1897.

cidal. "Populists cannot denounce the sins of the two old parties, and yet go into political copartnership with them," Georgia Populist Tom Watson warned Butler. "When we cease our war upon the two old parties, we have no longer any excuse for living."[20]

Following the election, antifusion or "mid-road" Populists demanded the reorganization of the National Committee to assure independent action in the future. Peffer joined in urging that a party conference be held, preferably coinciding with the February 22, 1897, meeting in Memphis of the National Reform Press Association, whose editors were inclined to oppose fusion. At first Butler attempted to conciliate the mid-roaders, even suggesting that Peffer be elected president of the NRPA to unify the party, but he refused to call a conference, which he feared would repudiate his leadership and the fusion policy he regarded as necessary. Working with Weaver, Simpson, and other advocates of fusion, Butler then moved to isolate his critics, whom he increasingly denounced. Peffer and other mid-roaders responded with their own attacks upon the regular party officials for "misusing their power," failing to protect Populist autonomy and integrity, and obstructing party reorganization. They called their own series of conferences in 1897 and 1898 "to save the party," as Peffer approvingly put it, by capturing "the party machinery." Convinced that serious differences separated Populists and Democrats and that Populist principles and objectives would not be advanced by submerging themselves in the Democratic party, mid-roaders also nominated separate antifusion Populist tickets in the state elections of 1897 and 1898.[21]

So believing, Peffer took a prominent role in campaigning in Iowa against Weaver and other Populists who supported a fusion ticket listed on the ballot only under the Democratic heading, a chilling sign to Peffer of the practical demise of the People's party.

20. C. Vann Woodward, *Tom Watson, Agrarian Rebel* (New York: Macmillan, 1938), 328; Rogers, *One-Gallused Rebellion*, 323–326.

21. Topeka *Advocate*, July 14, April 14, 1897; *Boston Herald*, January 11, 25, 1897.

If the fusion policy pursued by party leaders forced Populists to vote as members of the old parties, Peffer noted as early as 1897, "it would be more manly, more honorable, and more fitting every way to go as a volunteer Democrat or Republican than as a conscripted Populist." The results of these elections seemed to indicate that other Populists were coming to the same conclusion. Not only were the fusion tickets defeated, but the mid-road alternatives were virtually ignored when disaffected Populists, as Ignatius Donnelly reported, returned directly to the Republican party in order to gain "revenge on the Democrats who had invaded our ranks, bought up our leaders, and forced their loathsome nuptials on our unhappy people." Dissension over fusion, Peffer concluded, was causing "the Passing of the People's Party."[22]

With ever stronger language, Populist leaders in both Kansas and the nation denounced Peffer for creating discord within the fusion coalition. Convinced that the Democratic party had been thoroughly reformed in 1896, they argued that there was no need for an independent party. Indeed, Simpson even applied for a position on the Democratic National Congressional Committee. Peffer retorted that such permanent fusion under the Democratic leadership was "the way Jonah captured the whale," and plaintively urged "If our party is worth saving, let us fight for it under our own colors." His continued insistence that Democrats and Populists held different principles and objectives and his activities to prevent fusion provoked a torrent of what one editor termed "vituperation and abuse" from the fusionists that dominated both parties.[23]

22. Topeka *Advocate*, April 28, 1897; John D. Hicks, *The Populist Revolt: A History of the Farmers' Alliance and the People's Party* (Minneapolis: University of Minnesota Press, 1931), 396; William A. Peffer, "The Passing of the People's Party," *North American Review* 166 (January 1898): 12–23. For the Iowa campaign, see Peter H. Argersinger, "To Disfranchise the People: The Iowa Ballot Law and Election of 1897," *Mid-America* 63 (January 1981): 18–35.

23. Topeka *Advocate*, July 14, April 28, 1897; *Girard World*, October 7, 1897.

Increasingly isolated and under continual criticism, Peffer began to turn inward. After the 1897 election, he sold the Topeka *Advocate* and determined to withdraw from political life, returning to his agricultural, temperance, and literary interests of the past. He attempted to maintain a nominally nonpartisan attitude even when the Prohibition party nominated him for governor of Kansas in 1898. Furious with Populist Governor Leedy's refusal to enforce prohibition, a stratagem to retain Democrats in the fusion coalition, Peffer reluctantly accepted the nomination, but only as a private citizen for he insisted that he remained a Populist. His few campaign speeches were nonpartisan in nature and limited only to prohibition. A Topeka prohibitionist newspaper conceded that Peffer "was not nominated as a party Prohib and does not claim to be one," but it also aptly characterized Peffer's situation: "He claims to be a Populist, but it is a well known fact that he is . . . in reality a Populist without a party for the simple reason that the so-called Populist party are not populists, but fusionists first, last, and all the time." Indeed, Peffer contended that the party had left him, not the reverse. "The present Populist party will inevitably be absorbed in the Democratic party," he declared. "I am not a Democrat and I cannot follow the Populist party into the Democratic ranks."[24]

Peffer's separate candidacy was not responsible for the fusionist loss to the Republicans in the 1898 election, but many Populists again bitterly and viciously criticized Peffer for his course. After the election, Democrats and fusion Populists drew still closer together, thereby pushing Peffer further away. Permanent fusion, he announced, had effectively eliminated the People's party and forced Populists to choose between Republicans and Democrats, and "as between the Democratic and Republican parties I have always been against the Democrats." The press naturally reported that Peffer had returned to the GOP. This Peffer strenuously denied, asserting that he had made but two points: first, that the

24. Argersinger, *Populism and Politics*, 297–298.

People's party was dead and, second, that he was not a Democrat. "Now that the process of absorbing the Populist party is complete," he declared, "and the fight is between Republican and Democrat, I respectfully ask leave to be against the Democrat and stop there."[25]

Peffer's reasoning satisfied only himself. Populists and Democrats denounced him with what one newspaper called "a passion of rage," continuing the harsh criticism of recent years that had helped drive him from the People's party. Conversely, there was "music and dancing in the home of the G.O.P." as Republicans reached out to welcome him back.[26]

The *Chicago Tribune* seized the occasion to ask the former Senator to write "a history of the Populist party from its inception to the present day" for publication in its columns. Peffer agreed to do so and hurriedly wrote a narrative entitled *Populism, Its Rise and Fall*, which the *Tribune* published in the form of an extended series in May, June, and July 1899.[27] That account is republished for the first time in this book, making available an important document that has remained unknown and unused for too long.

This is a valuable work for many reasons, not the least because of Peffer's central importance in Populism and in the evolution of the People's party. Although Peffer wrote this account in the third person, it constitutes an insider's record prepared by perhaps the leading Populist figure. No other major Populist left such a memoir. Joseph Manning, an Alabama Populist, recounted his reminiscences in *Fadeout of Populism*, but this was a rambling survey written decades later, and Manning, although a noted Populist orator, was scarcely a prominent national figure in the party. Among Kan-

25. *Topeka State Journal*, May 18, 1899; *Topeka Daily Capital*, May 21, June 23, 1899.

26. Quotations in *Leavenworth Times*, May 23, 1899. The *Times* itself commented perceptively that "ex-Senator Peffer's return to the Republican party is not the forerunner but the belated consequence of Populist disintegration."

27. *Chicago Tribune*, May 28, 1899.

sas Populists, William F. Rightmire wrote two short accounts of his activities in organizing the party, but historians have disputed their accuracy and Rightmire had nothing to say about subsequent events. Few Populists, in fact, left any type of personal papers, a delinquency that has always hampered historians trying to understand the movement.[28] Thus, Peffer's *Populism, Its Rise and Fall*, a personal account of Populism and the People's party by its most prominent member, represents an extraordinary source for interested scholars of late nineteenth century politics and adds greatly to our knowledge of the whole movement. Moreover, although Peffer naturally emphasizes developments in Kansas, his reminiscences are national in scope and significance.

But, of course, Peffer's narrative is less—and more—than the complete history of Populism promised by the *Tribune*. As a personal account, it not only provides information about Peffer's experiences but it does so from Peffer's perspective—a perspective

28. Joseph C. Manning, *Fadeout of Populism: Pot and Kettle in Combat* (New York: Hebbons, 1928); W. F. Rightmire, "The Alliance Movement in Kansas—Origin of the People's Party," *Transactions of the Kansas State Historical Society* 9 (Topeka: State Printing Office, 1906), 1–8, and "Organization of the National People's Party," *Collections of the Kansas State Historical Society* 17 (Topeka: State Printing Office, 1928), 730–733. Rightmire's account is disputed in Robert C. McMath, Jr., "Preface to Populism: The Origin and Economic Development of the 'Southern' Farmers' Alliance in Kansas," *Kansas Historical Quarterly* 42 (Spring 1976): 55–65. Important manuscript collections survive for only a few Populists such as Ignatius Donnelly and Marion Butler. Peffer did accumulate massive files of letters, scrapbooks, and diaries covering four decades, and he obviously relied upon these papers in writing his memoir for he quotes frequently from letters and sometimes refers to their presence, as on page 84 below: "Within five feet of where these words are written lies a package of original letters of the character just described." Peffer later directed that his private papers be given to the Kansas State Historical Society, of which he was an officer, but his family divided the collection, nearly all of which was subsequently lost. The Society was able to acquire later several of the scrapbooks from Peffer's son, Douglas, but they contain little more than political cartoons, some of which appear as illustrations in this volume.

shaped not only by his own political and philosophical attitudes but by the bitter party in-fighting he had so recently endured. Indeed, the *Tribune* clearly approached Peffer with its own purposes in mind. A stalwart Republican newspaper, it obviously expected that Peffer's disaffection with his party's course and leadership would produce an account reflecting his own conclusions and perhaps persuasive to other wavering Populists.

The pedantic Peffer welcomed the opportunity. In agreeing to the *Tribune*'s proposal, Peffer outlined what he would write, declaring that he would explain the collapse of the People's party in order to inform "Republican writers and speakers" of Populist history and to save "as many as possible of the Populists of Republican antecedents . . . from the wreck." The ten chapters he originally planned ranged from one focused on the origins of the People's party, designed to explain, according to the *Tribune*, " 'What was the matter with Kansas' and other states West and South about 1890," to a final chapter consisting of an "appeal to Populists to avoid the Democratic party."[29] That two-sided approach, to provide factual information about the movement and to persuade Populists that neither their principles nor their interests were represented by the Democratic party, would be reflected in the entire memoir.

Only rarely does the second objective seriously interfere with the first, however. One possible such instance involves Peffer's attempt to estimate the relative proportions of former Republicans, Democrats, Union Laborites, and Prohibitionists among those discontented Kansans who combined in 1890 to create the People's party. This issue of the composition of the People's party according to partisan antecedents was an important one throughout the 1890s for it had obvious implications for party platforms, campaign tactics, and

29. *Chicago Tribune*, May 28, 1899. The *Tribune*'s reference was to the famous 1896 editorial by William Allen White, "What's the Matter with Kansas?" which ridiculed Populists, poor people, and "Pefferian speeches." For the full editorial, see *The Autobiography of William Allen White* (New York: Macmillan, 1946), 280–283.

the division of nominations to reflect the relative strength of each group in the coalition. In 1891, for example, W. H. T. Wakefield of Lawrence, Kansas, the 1888 vice-presidential nominee of the Union Labor party, declared that Union Laborites constituted the largest faction of Populists and the new party should choose a senator from their ranks rather than a former Republican like Peffer. In 1897, of course, Populists of Democratic antecedents insisted that Peffer be replaced by one from their own faction both to reflect their increased influence and to assure Democratic support for fusion. Nor were these concerns about partisan origins limited to Kansas Populists. As S. F. Norton, the Populist editor of the *Chicago Sentinel,* wrote to Colorado Populist leader Davis Waite, "the question of former *political affiliation*" was always crucial in making party nominations and decisions. Both Republicans and Democrats also took an interest in the partisan origins of their Populist opponents, and often made their own campaign decisions only after analyzing what the *Leavenworth Evening Standard* termed "the political antecedents of the men who were nominated by the People's Party." In the West, Republicans exaggerated the strength of former Democrats within the People's party in an attempt to frighten dissident Republicans into returning to the GOP rather than being dominated by and serving the purposes of Democrats; in the South, leading publicists reversed the proportions in attempting to depict the Populists as subservient to Republicans. Perhaps Peffer's calculations of the partisan composition of the 1890 Kansas Populist vote in this volume also had a political motive, for they vary from those he had originally made in 1890 by slightly decreasing the strength of Democrats and increasing the numbers of Republicans and other groups. Such a revision indirectly emphasizes how far the People's party had moved from its origins among discontented Republicans to its policy of apparently perpetual fusion with Democrats and suggests that "the Populists of Republican antecedents" should return home.[30]

30. Lawrence *Jeffersonian,* January 15, 1891; S. F. Norton to Davis Waite, August 28, 1895, Davis H. Waite Papers, Colorado State Archives

A more obvious and serious instance of how Peffer's situation in 1899 influenced his description of the history of Populism involves his effort to refurbish the image of Kansas Republicans and Senator John J. Ingalls in particular by writing that the party's platforms and Ingalls's "frequently expressed opinions" accorded with the principles of the Farmers' Alliance and that Peffer had been prepared to support Ingalls's reelection in 1890. There is virtually no basis for those statements. Ingalls himself, for instance, referred to the Farmers' Alliance as his "enemy" and "a secret organization based upon discontent, bound by oath, led by malevolent and vindictive conspirators." In 1890, moreover, Peffer had repeatedly denounced the conservative Ingalls for his indifference to popular distress and his statements that legislation could not relieve agricultural depression, a direct contradiction of the public position of both Peffer and the Alliance. The only attempt Ingalls ever made to speak in support of Alliance demands—his notorious "last chance" speech to appease furious farmers—Peffer had described at the time as "conceived in sin and brought forth in iniquity." Similarly, in here attempting to depict Kansas Republicans as advocates of financial reform, Peffer refers to their 1878 state platform favoring the retirement of national bank notes in favor of greenbacks, but he neglects to note that Kansas Democrats adopted the same plank in 1878, that the Republicans simultaneously denounced "irredeemable" paper money as intolerable "repudiation," and that by 1880 Kansas Republicans returned to economic

and Public Records, Denver; *Leavenworth Evening Standard*, June 17, 1892. Cf. Peffer's estimates given below, pp. 68–69, with those in William A. Peffer, *The Farmer's Side: His Troubles and Their Remedy* (New York: Appleton, 1891), 157. See *Topeka Daily Capital*, November 18, 1890, for a Republican estimate. Among historians who have made estimates and discussed their significance, see Clanton, *Kansas Populism*, 88; Argersinger, *Populism and Politics*, 73, 187–189; Scott G. McNall, *The Road to Rebellion: Class Formation and Kansas Populism, 1865–1900* (Chicago: University of Chicago Press, 1988), 243; and D. Scott Barton, "Party Switching and Kansas Populism," *Historian* 52 (May 1990): 453–467.

orthodoxy, endorsing specie resumption and never again supporting monetary reform beyond silver coinage. Ironically, in fact, in 1890 Peffer had cited the same 1878 Republican platform pledges in his effort to refute the argument that necessary reform could be accomplished through existing parties and to justify organizing a new one. Obviously, his political objectives shaped his writings: in 1890, he emphasized that the reform pledges had never been met; in 1899, he simply pointed out that they had been made.[31]

Such errors of omission are more troublesome and certainly more common than the simple misstatements about Ingalls, but they also provide valuable insight into Peffer's thinking and the Populists' predicament. Two areas are of particular note. First, Peffer provides little discussion in this volume about the origins of Populism, especially of the political context in which the People's party emerged. In Kansas, in particular, that context involved a failure on the part of the existing major parties to respond to the needs and demands of their rural constituents caught up in severe economic distress. That is to say, a third party is regarded as necessary only when existing parties fail to respond; it is not simply economic distress itself that generates third parties. Confronted with growing popular discontent, the Kansas GOP in 1888 had expediently pledged itself to a comprehensive agrarian reform program ranging from debtor relief to railroad regulation by adopting a platform that party leaders described as "an instruction from the party to each Republican member of the next legislature to favor the proposed legislation." But after sweeping to victory on these reform pledges, winning 160 of 165 seats in the 1889 legislature, the Republicans quickly repudiated their promises and voted down the reform program, leaving many Kansans convinced that a new party was

31. John J. Ingalls to P. I. Bonebreak, August 18, 1890, John J. Ingalls Papers, KSHS; *Kansas Farmer*, May 21, August 27, 1890, January 21, 1891. For Kansas party platforms, see Karl A. Svenson, "The Effect of Popular Dissent on Political Parties in Kansas" (Ph.D. diss., University of Iowa, 1948), 143–222. For Peffer's comments in this volume, see pp. 193–196.

necessary to achieve the desired goals. Peffer had been particularly outraged by this Republican failure, for as the editor of the *Kansas Farmer* he had been an important architect of the agrarian program. This Republican betrayal was the necessary condition for the creation of the People's party in the following year.[32]

By neglecting to mention the Republicans' failures and their indifference to the principles that prompted Populism, Peffer made easier his task of justifying a return to the GOP.[33] It also eliminated the need for him to demonstrate that the Republican party by the late 1890s had been reformed or changed and was now responsive to the issues it had previously spurned—something he would have found difficult to prove of a party that for a decade had opposed Populist demands for monetary inflation, an income tax, railroad regulation, electoral reforms, and other innovations on both the state and national levels and was then on the verge of passing the Gold Standard Act. This circumstance in turn made it possible for Peffer to argue in Chapter XII that the Democratic party had little in common with Populists without feeling it necessary to concede that Republicans often differed from Populists exactly as Democrats did.

This mode of writing may have reflected Peffer's continued attempt to convince himself and others that he opposed Democrats without being a Republican. Indeed, even after he began writing the series for the *Tribune*, Peffer still insisted that he had not returned to the GOP but had merely announced that he would never become a Democrat, that he had not left the People's party—it had

32. Argersinger, *Populism and Politics*, 12–21.
33. Peffer may also have neglected discussing in this volume the political context surrounding the creation of the People's party because of his reliance on his 1889 article that antedated independent political action and described the various farm orders, their grievances, and their objectives preceding the 1889 St. Louis meeting that attempted to unite them. For this article, indirectly cited in chapter one below, see William A. Peffer, "The Farmers' Defensive Movement," *Forum* 8 (December 1889): 464–473.

left him to join the Democrats.[34] Moreover, the arguments that Peffer advances in this volume about the differences between the "fundamental ideas" of Republicans and Democrats were not newly concocted out of literary expediency. He had consistently articulated them for years, and especially during the long struggle over the direction of the Populist party organization after the 1896 fusion campaign. In an interview with Isabel W. Ball in early 1897, for instance, Peffer had discussed in detail the points he makes in this book concerning the "fundamental ideas [that] may be taken as the foundation of the two great parties," which he characterized as a Republican commitment to "strong federal powers" and a Democratic commitment to "local self-government," and he had made the same condemnations of specific declarations in the 1896 Democratic platform. In 1898 he had repeatedly contrasted the Democratic commitment to a negative and limited government with Republican activism and had insisted that "as between the Democratic and Republican parties, with respect to their foundation beliefs concerning the powers and duties of our government, the Republican idea is much broader than that of the Democratic, and may, therefore, be expected to advance faster in improving the agencies of public operations."[35]

What was important about these earlier statements, however,

34. *Kansas Agitator* (Garnett), May 26, 1899. In his determined refusal to rejoin the Republican party, Peffer differed significantly from several other prominent Populists who shared his antipathy for the Democratic party and fusion. Some, such as Mary E. Lease of Kansas and Thomas F. Byron of Iowa, rejoined the GOP even in 1896, organizing McKinley Clubs and giving campaign speeches, rather than accept a national fusion with the Democrats. Others, such as the radical Henry L. Loucks of South Dakota, struggled against the fusionists until 1898 before repudiating what they saw as their debased Populist party and returning to the Republicans. Peffer continued to insist that he was not a Republican for several more years, although he did campaign for McKinley's reelection in 1900 on a nonpartisan basis.

35. *Kansas Semi-Weekly Capital*, February 2, 1897; Peffer, "Passing of the People's Party"; Topeka *Advocate and News*, November 23, 1898.

was Peffer's equally consistent conviction that Republicans were as much to be avoided as Democrats. Even as he described the dissolution of the People's party over fusion in 1898, for instance, and declared that antifusion Populists would not join the Democrats because the latter opposed an active national government, he had viewed the Bryan Democrats more favorably than the Republicans and had predicted that no Populists would join the GOP because Populist doctrines "are diametrically opposed to the principles and policies of the present Republican party."[36]

The question, then, of course, as Peffer himself recognized, was where were the antifusion Populists going? At first he thought they could go it alone, sidestepping Ball's charge that they would be only "a hopeless minority party" with the brave claim that "it will leave us where we were in the beginning."[37] But by 1899, Peffer had become convinced that Populism had been destroyed and that the consistent fusion policy had itself created a two-party system in which future political contests would be between Democrats and Republicans. In writing his history of Populism, then, he simply failed to mention the differences between Populists and Republicans, in effect acquiescing the flaws of the party he perceived as the lesser evil while continuing to attack the faults of the greater evil. The result of these omissions is to leave his readers with the impression that the GOP, at least in comparison with the Democratic party, was an appropriate destination for discontented Populists.[38] Only much later would Peffer himself take the final step and acknowledge that he had returned to the GOP, still insisting "I'm an insurgent though."[39]

36. Peffer, "Passing of the People's Party," 18.
37. *Kansas Semi-Weekly Capital*, February 2, 1897.
38. A nationalist in all things, Peffer was also clearly motivated in 1899 by the emergence of imperialism and the Democrats' efforts to make it a partisan issue. See *Topeka State Journal*, May 18, 1899, and Barry Hankins, "Manifest Destiny in the Midwest: Selected Kansans and the Philippine Question," *Kansas History* 8 (Spring 1985): 54–66.
39. *Kansas Semi-Weekly Capital*, February 2, 1897; Kansas Biographical Scrapbook, vol. 140, pp. 26–27, KSHS. For indications of Peffer's con-

These omissions do not, of course, weaken the value of this book; rather they illustrate the difficulties the Populists encountered in trying to overcome the burden of American politics. They also reflect aspects of the intense political culture of the time as well as the personal idiosyncrasies and attitudes of the author, just as would personal letters or interviews. Recognition of these matters is another step toward understanding the Populists.

Peffer's account also more directly reveals other important features of the Populist experience, some of which scholars have seriously neglected. One vivid example of the work's value is its information and insight into the subject of Populists in Congress, a topic nearly ignored by historians who have emphasized electoral politics at the state level.[40] As the party's first United States Senator, Peffer was in an ideal position to observe the attempts of its representatives in Congress to fashion a legislative program to implement the party's demands, to cooperate with sympathetic members of other parties, to publicize the party's principles, and to promote its organizational activities. In this capacity, he writes of the Populists' efforts and the obstacles and antagonists they encountered—

tinuing reform interests, see his following articles: "The Trust Problem and Its Solution," *Forum* 27 (July 1899): 523–533; "The Trust in Politics," *North American Review* 170 (February 1900): 244–252; "Fifty Years Ahead of Time: A Look Forward into the Political, Social, Industrial, and Labor Questions," Kansas Biographical Scrapbook, "P," vol. 14, p. 28, KSHS; "Government Banking," *North American Review* 191 (January 1910): 12–17. The final essay involves nearly pure economic Populism minus silver: government banking, paper money, government loans directly to the people at low rates of interest, deemphasis of the tariff, abolition of note-issuing national banks.

40. Exceptions to the neglect of Congressional analysis in Populist historiography include Gene Clanton, "'Hayseed Socialism' on the Hill: Congressional Populism, 1891–1895," *Western Historical Quarterly* 15 (April 1984): 139–162, and Peter H. Argersinger, "'No Rights on This Floor': Third Parties and the Institutionalization of Congress" (paper delivered at the Fifteenth Annual Meeting of the Social Science History Association, Minneapolis, October 20, 1990).

often placing his discussions in the context of one of the major themes of his narrative, that the growing importance of silver politics and the influence of Democrats disrupted the People's party and diverted its members from their original objectives. His descriptions of the Populist role in the Congressional maneuvering over proposed silver legislation as well as in tariff legislation and the enactment of the 1894 income tax are especially welcome. If one wishes for more detail about Peffer's own role in the conflict over the income tax, a legislative struggle in which both advocates and opponents regarded him as decisive, Peffer provides almost too much detail on the money question and the various forms it took in Congress, even quoting passages from proposed legislation. Finally, he also offers succinct and often perceptive evaluations of some of the major Populists he met in Washington—including Tom Watson of Georgia, William V. Allen of Nebraska, Marion Butler of North Carolina, and Sockless Jerry Simpson of Kansas, whose various commitments to Populist principles often appeared to Peffer to fluctuate during their tenure in Congress.

Also of particular interest are Peffer's observations on the political plans and activities of the leaders and officials of the People's party. Because party headquarters were in Washington, Peffer participated in numerous meetings with party officials in which campaign tactics and plans were debated and discussed, especially for the great 1896 election. The conflicts he had with James B. Weaver, William M. Stewart, and other fusionists figure prominently in this book.

Another significant feature of this book involves its several valuable discussions of behind-the-scenes maneuvering over the newspapers upon which the People's party depended for organizing and promoting its political work in Kansas and the nation. As a prominent editor as well as politician, Peffer was often involved in these crucial matters, and his $5,000 senatorial salary necessarily made him a financial backer for such publishing ventures among the otherwise poor Populists. Of particular importance to historians are his accounts of the meetings and activities of the National Reform

Press Association; the political scheming over three Topeka newspapers, the *Tribune*, the *Daily Press*, and the *Advocate*, the last of which he later acquired himself; and the creation and destruction of the *National Watchman*, the Populist newspaper he helped launch in Washington, D.C., to provide a national organ for the party. The *Watchman*'s fatal involvement in the various struggles over fusion and silver politics and its absorption by the *Silver Knight*, the major national newspaper of the silver movement, seem here to Peffer to presage the party's own fate.

Indeed, Peffer provides one of the most informative accounts about the important free silver movement that is available in any source, primary or secondary, offering a running commentary on the politics, personalities, organizational activities, journals, and finances of the silver movement.

There are still other areas upon which this book casts new light, including some of the financial arrangements among reformers, an important but unexplored topic. By reproducing various political documents, letters, speeches, and conversations not otherwise available, Peffer further enhances the historical value of this work. And Peffer's discussion of the "fundamental ideas" underlying the various parties is a valuable introduction to Populist ideology and attitudes toward government and the role of political parties and what might be expected of government.[41] These discussions about partisan differences in political attitudes and policies may prove as valuable and interesting as much of what Peffer has to say about developments within the People's party, Kansas politics, the silver movement, and the other topics he discusses, and they should contribute to our understanding of Populist ideology and of Populism's place in the reform tradition.

Finally, both directly and indirectly, this book illuminates a number of historiographical controversies. First, historians will find little

41. For a recent attempt to analyze some of Peffer's fundamental ideas, see Norman Pollack, *The Just Polity: Populism, Law, and Human Welfare* (Urbana: University of Illinois Press, 1987), 43–55, 322–331.

here to support the interpretation advanced by scholars in the 1950s that Populists were reactionary, nativistic, anti-Semitic, and irrational. This should not be surprising, for those characterizations were never based on serious research and have been effectively destroyed by subsequent scholarly investigations.[42] Peffer's focus on political developments rather than the economic origins of Populism also places this memoir outside the more recent scholarly discussions of the Farmers' Alliance and its contributions to the membership, structure, and ideology of the People's party or the role of cooperatives or the creation of a "movement culture."[43] But there is considerable material here to support the views of those historians who emphasize the destructive aspects of fusion politics and who reject the earlier view that free silver and fusion constituted the "climax of Populism" rather than its betrayal.[44] Moreover, Peffer's arguments about the ideological differences between Republicans and Democrats and between their counterparts within the Populist coalition find resonance in the work of those historians, primarily focused on Southern Populism, who stress the relative conservatism of Southern Populists of Democratic antecedents and their similarity to orthodox Democrats in their commitment to localism and limited government.[45]

42. For an assessment of the Populist historiography of the 1950s and early 1960s, see Theodore Saloutos, "The Professors and the Populists," *Agricultural History* 40 (October 1966): 235–254.

43. For examples of the new scholarship on the Farmers' Alliance, see Donna A. Barnes, *Farmers in Rebellion: The Rise and Fall of the Southern Farmers' Alliance and People's Party in Texas* (Austin: University of Texas Press, 1984), and Theodore Mitchell, *Political Education in the Southern Farmers' Alliance, 1887–1900* (Madison: University of Wisconsin Press, 1987).

44. For examples of the favorable view of fusion, see Robert F. Durden, *The Climax of Populism: The Election of 1896* (Lexington: University of Kentucky Press, 1965), and Norman Pollack, *The Populist Response to Industrial America* (Cambridge, Mass.: Harvard University Press, 1962). More critical of fusion are Argersinger, *Populism and Politics*, and Goodwyn, *Democratic Promise*.

45. For examples of the new scholarship on Southern Populism, see

Despite its importance, however, Peffer's *Populism, Its Rise and Fall* cannot be said to be great literature. It is, instead, the product of dramatic and astute journalism, composed by Kansas's most prominent political editor, at the request of a major national newspaper, and aimed at the contemporary public. It is written in his famous pedantic style, once aptly described by Walter Nugent as "sedate, logical, fact-crammed, humorless," and it reflects Peffer's noted study of history, political economy, and obscure government documents. It also reflects the observation of a contemporary reporter for the *Philadelphia Press* who noted that while Peffer had "the crazy notions of the Populists," he was a modest and "mild mannered gentleman . . . whose presentations of these notions has been made in the prosiest, least sensational manner imaginable."[46] Peffer not only wrote this account in the third person but apologized for referring to himself and sometimes succumbed to awkward phrasing in his attempts to avoid doing so.[47] One striking aspect of his writing is Peffer's evident conviction that his readers would find both interesting and comprehensible his detailed descriptions of financial legislation and would readily pore over vot-

Barton C. Shaw, *The Wool-Hat Boys: Georgia's Populist Party* (Baton Rouge: Louisiana State University Press, 1984), and Charles L. Flynn, Jr., "Procrustean Bedfellows and Populists: An Alternative Hypothesis," and Eric Anderson, "The Populists and Capitalist America: The Case of Edgecomb County, North Carolina," both in *Race, Class, and Politics in Southern History*, ed. Jeffrey J. Crow, Paul D. Escott, and Charles L. Flynn, Jr. (Baton Rouge: Louisiana State University Press, 1989), 81–105, 106–125.

46. Walter T. K. Nugent, *The Tolerant Populists: Kansas Populism and Nativism* (Chicago: University of Chicago Press, 1963), 63; Clanton, *Kansas Populism*, 294.

47. For Peffer's apology for "referring and alluding" to himself, see page 132. More typically, Peffer avoided mentioning his own name by using vague references to "the editor of the *Kansas Farmer*," "a Populist Senator," "the President of the Watchman Publishing Company," "a Kansan," or even "one of the gentlemen present." Virtually all such phrases in his narrative refer to Peffer himself, as do most passive constructions such as "it was argued" or "it was objected."

ing statistics for clues as to political developments. If modern readers do not find engrossing all such passages, they nevertheless will find much of value and interest in Peffer's important account of the rise and fall of Populism.

I
The Origin of the People's Party

The People's or Populist party of the United States had its origin in movements originally begun by farmers.

The war of the rebellion had devastated the Southern States, and in addition to other misfortunes of the people there money was extremely scarce. The national banking law taxed the state banks out of existence, and in the distribution of national bank circulation the South was poorly provided for. President [Andrew] Johnson in 1867 sent an employee of the Agricultural bureau South to investigate the condition of the farmers in that section, directing him to report any suggestions he should regard as remedial. Nothing ever came of his recommendations in the way of national legislation, but he thought an organization of the farmers for self-help and mutual protection would be a good thing, and he talked about it to some other government employees, several of whom were well up in Masonry and were good at ritualistic work. They conferred with a few outside persons, and finally seven men got together in Washington City and formed an association, to be known as the "Patrons of Husbandry," commonly designated the "Grange."

The project did not take well in the South. The farmers there were suspicious and stood aloof, but it took root in the Northern States and grew to ponderous proportions in a few years. All persons interested in agriculture were eligible to membership, and because of this latitude the order soon became top-heavy, and in 1874 the constitution was changed so as to cut off all persons not in some way directly identified in interest with farmers. The membership at that time was upwards of 800,000.

At the national council of 1874 a declaration of purposes was prepared and published, showing the object of the order to be "to labor for the good of our order, our country, and mankind." Among the many specific objects enumerated are these:

> To develop a better and higher manhood and womanhood among ourselves; to maintain inviolate our laws; to reduce our expenses; to diversify our crops; to condense the weight of our exports; to discountenance the credit system, the mortgage system, the fashion system, and every other system tending to prodigality and bankruptcy. We propose in meeting together, talking together, working together, buying together, selling together, and, in general, acting together for our mutual protection and advancement, as occasion may require.

These are only part of the specific objects mentioned. Proceeding, they declare further:

> We desire to bring producers and consumers, farmers and manufacturers, into the most direct and friendly relations possible. Hence we must dispense with a surplus of middlemen. . . . In our noble order there is no communism, no agrarianism. We are not enemies of capital, but we oppose the tyranny of monopolies. We are opposed to excessive salaries, high rates of interest, and exorbitant per cent profits in trade.

There is much more, but these are sufficient to show both the social and commercial side of the Grange. But the order did not long retain its abnormal growth. With the long and disastrous depression following the panic of 1873 the Grange rapidly diminished in membership and influence, but the faithful thousands that remained have prospered and are now a compact body of well-to-do, intelligent farmers.[1]

While the Grange was declining other bodies of farmers in other parts of the country were organizing. In 1879, in Texas, some farmers got together and formed an alliance, which, in the course of ten years, extended all over the Southern States, and was fast spreading into the Northwestern region, more especially in Kansas. After absorbing several other similar bodies its name became "The Farmers' Alliance and Industrial Union." The objects, purposes, ambitions, and principles were much like those of the Patrons of Husbandry. It began with the following declaration of principles:

1. To labor for the education of agricultural classes in the science of economical government, in a strictly nonpartisan spirit.
2. To develop a better state mentally, morally, socially, and financially.
3. To create a better understanding for sustaining civil officers maintaining law and order.
4. Constantly to strive to secure entire harmony and good-will among all mankind and brotherly love among ourselves.
5. To suppress personal, local, sectional, and national prejudices, all unhealthy rivalry, and all selfish ambition.

To these were added, later, objects on charitable and benevolent lines, to look after the widow and fatherless, to assuage and relieve distress, etc.

> To exercise charity toward offenders, to construe words and deeds in their most favorable light, granting honesty of purpose and good intentions to others; and to protect the principles of the Alliance unto death. Its laws are reason and equity,

---

1. For a valuable study of the Grange, see D. Sven Nordin, *Rich Harvest: A History of the Grange, 1867–1900* (Jackson: University Press of Mississippi, 1974).

its cardinal doctrines inspire purity of thought and life, and its intentions are "peace on earth and good will toward men."

In 1890, when the Alliance had attained its largest proportions, its voting membership was estimated at 2,500,000.

In 1880, at Chicago, another organization was formed under the name of "National Farmers' Alliance," resulting from a local movement in that city begun three years before by the editor of the *Western Rural*. The object of the body was, among other things:

> To unite the farmers of the United States for their protection against class legislation, the encroachments of concentrated capital, and the tyranny of monopoly; to provide against being imposed upon by swindlers and swindling advertisements in the public prints; to oppose, in our respective political parties, the election of any candidate to office, State or national, who is not thoroughly in sympathy with the farmers' interests; to demand that the existing political parties shall nominate farmers, or those who are in sympathy with them, for all offices within the gift of the people, and to do anything in a legitimate manner that may serve to benefit the producer.

This body grew to about 400,000 members in a few years.

The Farmers' Mutual Benefit Association originated in Southern Illinois in 1887 and spread rapidly South, East, and West. It was quite largely represented in Kentucky, Missouri, and Kansas, as well as in Illinois and Indiana.

The objects of these several associations of farmers, though stated in different language, were substantially the same. All of them transacted their business in secret. The Chicago movement started as an open body, but afterwards changed to a secret order. Three features in all these farmer movements are conspicuous—

namely: (1) the objects assigned; (2) the national loyalty of the membership; and (3) the high moral tone of their official literature.

A magazine writer in 1889 said: "The origin of the farmers' movement is found in the operation of three of the most powerful and active agencies in modern civilization—railroads, middlemen, and banks."[2] The rehabilitation of the South and the settlement of the great West set in motion new forces which soon resulted in an enormous indebtedness, and when the bottom fell out of the boom a great many thousand people found themselves adrift; and as part of the history of the times, these great secret associations of farmers form an interesting chapter.

In 1889 a general call was issued inviting delegates from all farmers' associations in the country to meet at St. Louis in December of that year for the purpose of effecting a union of all in one body. The Knights of Labor and other industrial organizations were likewise invited to attend and take part in the proceedings.

The December meeting was held, but the only bodies participating were the Farmers' Alliance and Industrial Union and the Knights of Labor. A committee on demands, representing both orders, was appointed, and the following, known as the "seven demands," were laid before the joint committee:

1. We demand the abolition of national banks and the substitution of legal tender treasury notes in lieu of national bank notes, issued in sufficient volume to do the business of the country on a cash system, regulating the amount needed on a per capita basis, as the business interests of the country expand; and that all money issued by the government shall be legal tender in payment of all debts, both public and private.
2. We demand the free and unlimited coinage of silver.

2. Peffer here quotes from page 464 of his own essay, "The Farmers' Defensive Movement," *Forum* 8 (December 1889): 464–473.

3. We demand that Congress shall pass such laws as shall effectually prevent the dealing in futures of all agricultural and mechanical productions, preserving such a stringent system of procedure in trials as shall secure prompt conviction and imposing such penalties as shall secure the most perfect compliance with the law.

4. We demand the passage of laws prohibiting alien ownership of land, and that Congress take early steps to devise some plan to obtain all lands now owned by aliens and foreign syndicates, and that all lands now held by railroads or other corporations in excess of such as are actually used and needed by them, be reclaimed by the government and held for actual settlers only.

5. Believing in the doctrine of "equal rights for all and special privileges to none," we demand that taxation, national or State, shall not be used to build up one interest or class at the expense of another. We believe that the money of the country should be kept as much as possible in the hands of the people, and hence we demand that all revenues, national, State, or county, shall be limited to the necessary expenses of the government, economically and honestly administered.

6. We demand that Congress provide for the issue of a sufficient amount of fractional paper currency to facilitate exchange through the medium of the United States mail.

7. We demand that the means of communication and transportation shall be owned by and operated in the interest of the people, as is the United States postal system.

The joint committee reported these demands as their unanimous agreement. The report was signed, on the part of the Farmers' Alliance, by S. B. Erwin, chairman, and U. S. Hall, secretary, and B. H. Clover of Kansas, with sixteen others; and on the part of the Knights of Labor by T. V. Powderly, A. W. Wright, and Ralph

Beaumont.[3] B. H. Clover, who signed the report, was at the time President of the Kansas State Farmers' Alliance.[4]

3. S. B. Erwin of Clinton, Kentucky, was the Kentucky State President of the National Farmers' Alliance and Industrial Union and the editor of the *Kentucky State Union* newspaper. Uriel S. Hall of Hubbard, Missouri, was the Missouri State President of the Farmers' Alliance. A conservative Democrat who bitterly opposed the subtreasury and the creation of a third party, Hall used the Missouri Alliance to protect the Democratic party and gain election to Congress in 1892 and 1894. Benjamin H. Clover of Cambridge, Kansas, was the Kansas State President of the Farmers' Alliance. As a disgruntled Republican farmer, Clover had helped organize a successful local "People's party" in Cowley County in 1889. In 1890 he would lead in the creation of the famous state People's party and be elected to Congress. Terence V. Powderly of Pennsylvania was the Grand Master Workman of the Knights of Labor, the nation's largest labor organization. Although he sometimes engaged in radical rhetoric and attended the 1891 Cincinnati conference that launched the national People's party, Powderly was relatively conservative and determined to prevent his organization from being committed to a third party. By 1894 he was an ardent Republican and reviled by many of his former labor associates. A. W. Wright was one of the most skilled negotiators of the Knights of Labor. In October 1889, he had represented the organization in its discussions with the rival American Federation of Labor to resolve conflicts within the labor movement; the December 1889 meeting at St. Louis was the first of a series of conferences in which he met with the various farm orders. He attended the famous 1890 Ocala conference of the Farmers' Alliance, for example, and at the St. Louis meeting of the Confederation of Industrial Organizations in February 1892 he chaired the subcommittee on land reform. Ralph Beaumont was the national lecturer of the Knights of Labor and the head of the organization's lobbying bureau in Washington, D.C. A socialist, Beaumont would henceforth work closely with Alliance radicals and Populists, edit the newspaper of the National Citizens' Alliance, an organization to spread Populism into the cities, and serve on the executive committee of the National Reform Press Association.

4. For more complete accounts of the Farmers' Alliance, its organizational development, and its crucial significance in the origins of Populism, see Robert C. McMath, Jr., *Populist Vanguard: A History of the Southern Farmers' Alliance* (Chapel Hill: University of North Carolina Press, 1975), and Lawrence Goodwyn, *Democratic Promise: The Populist Moment in America* (New York: Oxford University Press, 1976).

The first effective movement toward the formation of the Populist party was begun in Kansas. In common with the people of the Northwest at that time, Kansas farmers had lost heavily in various ways, but chiefly from overspeculation, exorbitant rates of interest, excessive railroad charges, and depreciation of values. In 1884-85 prices of sheep, cattle, and horses started downward, and wheat kept these company. The total number of livestock in the State in 1884 was 5,544,391, in which number 1,206,297 sheep were included. By 1890 the sheep had diminished by nearly a million head—exactly 924,643. This loss in number was nearly made up by other and much more valuable classes of animals, the total number that year being 5,639,476; but the aggregate value was $2,111,708 less than that of the larger number, including sheep, in 1884.

While corn and oats had fairly well maintained their record during the decade, the aggregate wheat production of the five years, 1885 to 1889, was 45 per cent less than that of the last preceding five years, and its value was 51 per cent less.

The population of the State was increased about half a million during the first eight years of the '80s, and twenty-three counties in the western half of the State had been settled in the meantime. A heavy indebtedness had been incurred in the purchase and improvement of land.

As it was in other agricultural States, so it was in Kansas. Times were hard, and in addition to other misfortunes the State was overrun with a horde of conscienceless speculators, who were defrauding us and swindling their correspondents. We were heavily in debt, and creditors, as usual when times are hardest, are most anxious about collecting their debts or obtaining additional security. This anxiety resulted here, as elsewhere, in depressing land values and forcing sales needlessly. Naturally, there was much dissatisfaction and unrest. Everybody thought there was something wrong, and a great many people in looking about for causes and remedies attributed the general depression to legislation or the lack of it. Such were the conditions all over the South and in the new States west of the Mississippi River at the closing of the year 1889.

During December of that year and running through January following, a series of articles under the heading, "The Way Out," appeared in the *Kansas Farmer*, an agricultural paper which was in full sympathy with the Alliance movement and advocated all the principles, purposes, and demands of the order.[5] "The Way Out" proposed a system of government paper money, to be loaned at 1 per cent to people whose homes were mortgaged, taking the same security that the present private lenders had taken. The author estimated that $500,000,000 would be enough, when managed through government agencies, to redeem every home in the country then in danger. The demand for "The Way Out" was so great that the matter had to be put in pamphlet form, and it ran into the thirteenth edition.[6]

The Kansas State Farmers' Alliance at that time numbered about 100,000 voters. Half of them, probably, read the *Kansas Farmer*. That paper had long been urging farmers to organize themselves, so that if they could not control the parties to which they belonged and thus secure the legislation they desired, they could form a party of their own and strive for success in that way.

The term for which Senator Ingalls of Kansas[7] had last been elected would expire with the third day of March, 1891, and his

5. Peffer was the editor of the *Kansas Farmer* and the author of "The Way Out," an important forerunner to his later book, *The Farmer's Side: His Troubles and Their Remedy* (New York: Appleton, 1891), the primary expression of the early Populist positions on economics, society, and politics.

6. The influence, as well as the popularity, of Peffer's pamphlet seemed remarkable to some observers. In attempting to explain the subsequent astonishing election of 1890, which saw not only the birth of Populism in the West but unprecedented political upheavals in other regions as well, the *Topeka Capital* concluded that perhaps a popular reaction against the McKinley Tariff had produced the election upsets elsewhere, "but what did it in Kansas was 'The Way Out.' " *Topeka Daily Capital*, November 12, 1890.

7. John James Ingalls of Atchison, Kansas, was the state's leading Republican, a three-term United States Senator, and the president pro tempore of the Senate. A brilliant "bloody shirt" orator but a callous cynic

successor would be chosen by the Legislature to be elected in November, 1890. The Senator was popular in Kansas and had a great many friends in the Alliance. In view of the general unrest and the rapid spread of farmers' associations, it became important to have definite information with respect to the views of Mr. Ingalls touching the demands of the Farmers' Alliance; and for the purpose of procuring such information the editor of the *Kansas Farmer* in February addressed a letter to Senator Ingalls, submitting certain questions, and requesting answers to them for publication. These were the questions:

1. What legislation, if any, do you recommend by way of relief to farmers in the present depressed condition of agriculture?
2. Do you favor an increase in the volume of circulating money? If yes, to what extent, in what way do you propose to effect the change and how get the money in circulation?
3. In what respect, if at all, and for what purpose, do you favor changing the national banking law?
4. Do you favor free and unlimited coinage of silver at present weight and fineness?

The editor's letter was promptly and politely acknowledged, but that was the end of the correspondence. The questions were never answered, and after waiting three months without answer the *Kansas Farmer*, in May following, came out in an editorial opposing the re-election of Mr. Ingalls.

The next month a conference was held among Alliance men and members of the Union Labor party, when arrangements were made for calling a State convention in August for putting out a full State

who unmercifully ridiculed reformers along with Democrats, Ingalls was unconcerned with the questions that troubled his rural constituents. Benjamin Clover, for instance, skewered Ingalls's personal policy of "skinning Democrats" to divert attention from pressing issues by noting that Democratic "skins are the thinnest clothing a shivering family was ever wrapped up in." Topeka *Advocate*, May 21, 1890.

ticket, and for the nomination of candidates for Congress, for county offices, and members of the Lower House of the Legislature. The Senators elected in 1888 held over.

At the August 13th convention the People's party of the State of Kansas was organized, and the State ticket then named came within 6,000 votes of success. The candidate for Attorney General, being also on the Democratic ticket, was elected by a large majority. Ninety-six out of 125 members of the State Legislature were elected, with five of the eight Congressmen to which the State was entitled.[8]

Among the persons elected to Congress was B. H. Clover, who at the time was President of the Kansas State Farmers' Alliance and Industrial Union, and who, with other active members of the new party, attended the meeting of the Grand Council of the Farmers' Alliance and Industrial Union held at Ocala, Florida, in December following the Kansas election; and so enthusiastic were they and others who met at Ocala from different parts of the country that a movement was then set on foot to call a national conference, some time in the near future, to consider whether the time was not ripe for the formation of a national party on lines of the "seven demands" laid down by the Alliance at St. Louis.

In pursuance of the agreement at Ocala, a call was published some weeks afterward, issuing from Kansas,[9] for a national conference to be held at Cincinnati May 19, 1891, at which time and place

8. See pages 57–71 for a discussion of the 1890 Kansas campaign and the election of Peffer to the United States Senate. For scholarly studies that analyze these subjects in greater detail, see Peter H. Argersinger, "Road to a Republican Waterloo: The Farmers' Alliance and the Election of 1890 in Kansas," *Kansas Historical Quarterly* 33 (Winter 1967): 443–469; Peter H. Argersinger, "The Most Picturesque Drama: The Kansas Senatorial Election of 1891," ibid. 38 (Spring 1972): 43–64; and O. Gene Clanton, *Kansas Populism: Ideas and Men* (Lawrence: University Press of Kansas, 1969), 73–90.

9. Although the call for the Cincinnati Conference was signed by some national reform leaders, such as Ignatius Donnelly, James B. Weaver, and S. F. Norton, the project was primarily a Kansas undertaking. W. F. Right-

there gathered 1,417 delegates, representing the Alliance and other farmers' organizations, Knights of Labor, and other bodies of workingmen, from thirty-three States, Kansas leading with 411 delegates, followed by Ohio with 317, Indiana with 154, Nebraska with 94, Illinois with 88, Missouri with 73, Kentucky with 59, Minnesota with 30, Texas with 26, Wisconsin with 21, West Virginia with 13, South Dakota with 10, New York, Massachusetts, and Pennsylvania with 8 each, Tennessee, Arkansas and the District of Columbia each with 6, Washington and Wyoming with 4 each, Colorado with 3, Alabama, Florida, Georgia, Louisiana, and Maine with 2 each, and Connecticut, North Carolina, North Dakota, Rhode Island, and South Carolina with 1 each.

Kansas, having the largest delegation present, was honored by the selection of her lately elected United States Senator to preside over the deliberations of the conference.

The Committee on Resolutions reported the following, which was adopted unanimously:

1. That in view of the great social, industrial, and economical revolution now dawning upon the civilized world and the new and living issues confronting the American people, we believe that the time has arrived for a crystallization of the political reform forces of our country and the formation of what should be known as the People's party of the United States of America.

mire of Topeka, the unsuccessful 1890 Populist candidate for chief justice of the Kansas Supreme Court and, in 1891, the secretary of the National Citizens' Alliance, drew up and issued the call for a conference, and it was signed by newly elected Populist Senator Peffer of Topeka; P. P. Elder of Franklin County, the Populist Speaker of the Kansas House of Representatives; S. W. Chase, the chair of the Populist state executive committee; Henry Vincent of Winfield, the editor of the Populist newspaper, the *American Nonconformist*, and other leading Kansas Populists. See W. F. Rightmire, "Organization of the National People's Party," *Collections of the Kansas State Historical Society* 17 (Topeka: State Printer, 1928), 730–733; *Topeka Daily Capital*, February 8, 1891.

This Republican cartoon depicts the new People's party organized in Cincinnati in 1891 as a patchwork affair of many different dissident groups, with the obvious implication that it would not long hold together. Aloft with Peffer on a "platform of lunacy" are Terence Powderly of the Knights of Labor, Benjamin Butler, the 1884 Greenback presidential candidate, and Kansas Populist Jerry Simpson. (Judge, June 6, 1891)

2. That we most heartily indorse the demands of the platforms as adopted at St. Louis, Missouri, in 1889; Ocala, Florida, in 1890; and at Omaha, Nebraska,[10] in 1891, by the industrial organizations there represented, summarized as follows:

Then followed the seven demands adopted at St. Louis in 1889, with these additions, as they were adopted at Ocala and Omaha:

We demand a just and equitable system of graduated tax on income.

We demand the most rigid, honest, and just national control and supervision of the means of public communication and transportation; and if this control and supervision do not remove the abuses now existing we demand the government ownership of such means of communication and transportation.

We demand the election of the President and Vice-President and United States Senators by a direct vote of the people.

The other resolutions provide machinery for calling a national convention in 1892 for the purpose of forming a new party. A central committee was appointed to arrange for a meeting with such other similar committees of industrial bodies as were in sympathy with this movement at St. Louis, February 22, 1892, to call a national nominating convention to organize the new party, declare its principles, and name its candidates for President and Vice-President of the United States.[11]

10. The National (or "Northern") Farmers' Alliance met in Omaha in January 1891. Its platform resolutions were similar to those of the National Farmers' Alliance and Industrial Union (or "Southern Alliance"), although with a greater emphasis on political or electoral reform, and it was more prepared to countenance a national third party.

11. For a more detailed description of the Cincinnati conference and

*Although Peffer never sought a presidential nomination, his stature in the People's party made him a logical choice to many Americans, cartoonists included. Here Peffer is portrayed as an eager presidential aspirant, along with Democratic Senator Arthur Gorman of Maryland, former President Grover Cleveland, Democratic Governor David Hill of New York, Russell Alger, the Republican former governor of Michigan, Republican Senator Shelby Cullom of Illinois, and Democratic Governor James Campbell of Ohio. (*Judge, August 8, 1891*)*

The St. Louis committee conference resulted in a call for a national convention to be held at Omaha July 4, 1892, and at that place and time the People's party of the United States was formed, a national platform of principles adopted, and James B. Weaver of Iowa and James G. Field of Virginia, both members of the

Peffer's leading role in it, see Larry G. Osnes, "The Birth of a Party: The Cincinnati Populist Convention of 1891," *Great Plains Journal* 10 (Fall 1970): 11–24.

Farmers' Alliance, were nominated as the new party's candidates
for President and Vice-President.[12]

12. James B. Weaver was a veteran reformer and inflationist who had
been the 1880 presidential nominee of the National Greenback party and,
through fusion with the Democrats, had been elected to three terms in
Congress during the 1870s and 1880s. As a Western Populist with a notable
Civil War military record as a brevetted general in the Union Army, Weaver
was balanced on the ticket by ex-Confederate veteran James G. Field of
Virginia, whose title of "General" was only a courtesy. The nomination of
Field, a relatively conservative farmer and lawyer who did not commit himself to the People's party until the eve of the Omaha convention, was an attempt by the Populists to neutralize the politics of sectionalism and attract
Southern support. One historian has described the nomination of "this
rather typically old-school gentleman" as "largely owing to the fact that
the new party was too young to be thoroughly acquainted with its own con-
stituency." William DuBose Sheldon, *Populism in the Old Dominion: Virginia Farm Politics, 1885-1900* (Princeton, N.J.: Princeton University
Press, 1935), 85.

II
Southern Democrats, the Farmers' Alliance, and Independent Politics

The Farmers' Alliance and Industrial Union was founded among Democrats by members of the Democratic party. The order was to be strictly non-partisan and it was not difficult to maintain that status in the far South, where all the people that took part in social and political affairs belonged to one party. The members of the Alliance were all white people and Democrats. Permission was granted to colored people to form alliances of their own and a few were organized; they conferred with their white brethren, but they had no influence, and it was not intended that they should have.[1]

1. Peffer here refers to the intentions of Southern Democrats toward potential black influence and not his own attitude. In the early 1890s, he repeatedly maintained that the Farmers' Alliance and the Populists in Kansas made no racial distinctions and urged the South to act likewise, realizing that the interests of the oppressed transcended race. Populists, he added, opposed as much the politicians' attempts to incite racial prejudice as sectional hatred, for both were used to divert popular attention from economic exploitation. See, for example, William A. Peffer, "The Farmers' Alliance," *Cosmopolitan* 10 (April 1891): 699; *Kansas Farmer* (Topeka), November 26, 1890. For a scholarly analysis of the Kansas situation, see William H. Chafe, "The Negro and Populism: A Kansas Case Study," *Journal of Southern History* 34 (August 1968): 402–419. For the tragic career of the so-called Colored Farmers' Alliance in the South, see William F. Holmes, "The Demise of the Colored Farmers' Alliance," ibid. 41 (May 1975): 187–200. For a study that contrasts Peffer's surprisingly liberal ra-

Naturally it was expected that, on account of the non-partisan character of the Alliance and because of the uniform Democracy of its membership in the Southern States, the recruits from more northern latitudes, when they came under the softening influences of non-partisan aroma wafted on Southern breezes, would cast off their political garments and put on the uniform of the army in which they enlisted.

The *National Economist*, published in Washington City by Dr. C. W. Macune,[2] an able man, was the organ of the Farmers' Alliance. It was well conducted, had a wide circulation, and wielded a powerful influence among the Southern farmers. Dr. Macune was President of the Texas State Alliance, and it was on his recommendation that a union was formed with the Farmers' Union of Louisiana, the Agricultural Wheel of Arkansas, and other local bodies, ending finally in the formation of the largest body ever known. Its membership in 1891 was estimated at upward of 4,000,000, three-fifths of whom were voters and 85 per cent of them lived in Southern States.

The *National Economist* insisted on maintaining the non-parti-

cial attitudes with those of Southern Democrats in an earlier period, see Peter H. Argersinger, "The Conservative as Radical: A Reconstruction Dilemma," *Tennessee Historical Quarterly* 34 (Summer 1975): 168–187.

2. Dr. Charles W. Macune was the organizational genius behind the Southern Alliance. Physician, lawyer, editor, and economic theorist, he was an economic radical and a social and political conservative. The originator of several Alliance projects, from the Texas Alliance Exchange, which he served as business manager, to the famous subtreasury concept, he also served at various times as national president of the Southern Farmers' Alliance, chair of the Alliance's legislative committee in Washington, editor of the organization's national newspaper, the *National Economist*, and president of the National Reform Press Association. Macune nevertheless remained committed to the Democratic party and opposed any third party tendencies within the Alliance. He did not have, as Lawrence Goodwyn has concluded, "the political courage of his economic convictions." Goodwyn, *Democratic Promise: The Populist Moment in America* (New York: Oxford University Press, 1976), 563.

san feature and its editor, in his public addresses, urged the importance of this matter. The national lecturer, Mr. Terrell of Texas,[3] followed in the same vein and urged this characteristic of the order upon the attention of Kansas people when he came to talk Alliance to them. And when Colonel Polk of North Carolina,[4] National President, came north on the same errand, he taught the same doctrine. Colonel Livingston of Georgia[5] spoke in like manner. And when the matter of forming a new party was agitated in Kansas all

3. Ben Terrell of Texas was a former Confederate soldier and farmer who helped organize the National (Southern) Farmers' Alliance in 1887 and was then elected its National Lecturer five times in the next seven years. A close ally of Macune, Terrell long favored a nonpartisan course for the Alliance but moved fitfully toward independent political action. He was the president of the Confederation of Industrial Organizations, which met in St. Louis on February 22, 1892, and implicitly endorsed the People's party organized in Cincinnati in 1891. Terrell was then elected to a committee to confer with the executive committee of the People's party to call a national nominating convention. At this convention, held in Omaha on July 4, 1892, Terrell was runner-up to James G. Field of Virginia in balloting for the Populist nomination for vice-president.

4. Leonidas L. Polk had for years been a prominent leader in Southern agriculture. He had been an active Granger, the founder of the North Carolina State Agricultural Department, the editor of the *Progressive Farmer*, and a moving force in the establishment of a state agricultural college. When the Farmers' Alliance entered North Carolina in 1887, Polk joined it enthusiastically and was elected vice-president in 1887, chair of the national executive committee in 1888, and president in 1889. He initially opposed independent political action by the Alliance, but personally endorsed Populist candidates in Kansas in 1890 and by 1891 was maneuvering the Alliance toward the third party. A good speaker and personally popular, this former Confederate of Unionist sentiments was the ideal candidate for the Populists in their fight against the politics of sectionalism and almost certainly would have received their nomination for the presidency in 1892. Unfortunately, he died suddenly shortly before the Omaha Convention. Peffer had become a close friend and served as a pall bearer.

5. Leonidas F. Livingston, a small planter from Newton County, Georgia, was a volatile and ambitious politician who served as president of the Georgia Farmers' Alliance and was elected to Congress as an Alliance Democrat in 1890. But he was the leader of those described as Democrats

these distinguished Alliance men expressed the wish that the [party] movement would not extend beyond the boundaries of that State.

The new national party agitation did not begin in the South. It was not until after the successful revolution in Kansas and its phenomenal work in the short campaign of 1890, and the visit of Kansas people at Ocala, that the contagion took root and began to spread there. And its growth was slow among Southern Alliance men at first. They all voted the Democratic ticket in 1890, as they had been doing in past years. Their Alliance doctrines did in no way interfere with their party views, at least not enough to impel them to change their votes on election day.

The total vote for Governor in Alabama in 1890 was 139,910, and the Democratic majority was 95,989, or 76 per cent of the whole vote cast. Republicans and Prohibitionists cast all the rest of the votes. The same year in Georgia the Democratic candidate for Governor had no opposition. He received 105,365 votes—all that were polled. At the Presidential election two years before the total vote was 100,499. At the Gubernatorial election in Texas in 1890 the Democratic candidate received a majority of 181,594 out of a

---

first and Alliancemen second. He steadfastly opposed any break from the Democratic party and even tried to rescind the charters of any suballiances that approved the reform demands of the 1892 St. Louis meeting of the Confederation of Industrial Organizations. He infuriated Peffer with his statement that "we don't care what they do in Kansas and other western states. They can have a third party if they want one; in fact, a third party in Kansas is probably a good thing with which to overthrow the Republican party, and in that good work we wish them success; but in the South we want no third party" (quoted in *Topeka Daily Capital*, February 9, 1892). His opportunism, however, also alienated many Southerners, and one Georgia suballiance condemned him as "Benedict Arnold Judas Iscariot Livingston" and demanded that the Farmers' Alliance remove him as its state president and "with a pole long enough to keep the odorous dead cat from our nostrils . . . gently lift it over the garden wall, and consign it to its proper sphere—among the scum and Wall Street pimps of the so-called Democratic party." Quoted in Barton C. Shaw, *The Wool-Hat Boys: Georgia's Populist Party* (Baton Rouge: Louisiana State University Press, 1984), 44.

total of 343,270. The rest of the votes were cast by Republicans and Prohibitionists.

There were some Alliance men in Southern States elected to Congress in 1890, and General Gordon[6] owed his election as United States Senator the same year to the Alliance people. Senator Irby of South Carolina[7] was President of the State Alliance. His election was wholly due to the influence of that order and the votes of its members at the country polling places and in the Legislature.

When the Fifty-second Congress convened in December, 1891, it was in order for the Alliance members North and South to count noses and take counsel together. Georgia had sent up three Alliance members—Mr. Livingston, Mr. Moses,[8] and Mr. Winn.[9] In the brief biographical sketches of these gentlemen contained in the

6. John B. Gordon was a Confederate general, wealthy speculator, railroad promoter, corporate lawyer, and Democratic politician. A member of Georgia's so-called "Bourbon Triumvirate," he had previously served as a United States Senator from 1873 to 1880 and as governor of Georgia from 1886 to 1890. Despite his conservative attitudes and hostility to the subtreasury, he was again elected to the Senate in 1890 by a legislature dominated by Alliance Democrats. For a valuable analysis of that peculiar election, which stresses the conservative nature of the Alliance Democrats led by Livingston, see William F. Holmes, "The Southern Farmers' Alliance and the Georgia Senatorial Election of 1890," *Journal of Southern History* 50 (May 1984): 197–224.

7. John L. M. Irby of Laurens, South Carolina, a lawyer and noted political manipulator, was the chief lieutenant of the unscrupulous Democratic leader, Benjamin R. Tillman. Irby had been a member of the South Carolina legislature since 1886, serving as speaker in 1890, and as Democratic state chair in 1890 he had worked with Tillman to control and limit the influence of the Farmers' Alliance. Irby's election to the Senate in 1890 was his reward for such service.

8. Charles L. Moses of Turin, Georgia, was a farmer and member of the Farmers' Alliance. He was elected to Congress in 1890 as an Alliance Democrat and thereafter vigorously opposed the People's party. He was reelected to Congress in 1892 and 1894 as a regular Democrat.

9. Thomas E. Winn was a farmer and school commissioner in Gwinnett County, Georgia, until elected to Congress as an Alliance Democrat in 1890. He refused to join the Populist congressional caucus in 1891, believ-

Congressional Directory, it appears that Colonel Livingston was, at the time of this election, "President of the Georgia State Alliance," and that he "was elected to the Fifty-second Congress as a Democrat." As to Mr. Moses, the directory shows that he "is a member of the Farmers' Alliance" and that he "was elected to the Fifty-second Congress as a Democrat." In the case of Mr. Winn, his sketch shows that he "was elected to the Fifty-second Congress as an Alliance man and Democrat." Thomas E. Watson, also a member from Georgia, "was elected to the Fifty-second Congress as a Democrat." The directory sketch shows further that Mr. Watson "was Democratic Elector for the State at large in 1888;" that "beside the practice of law he has been, and still is, largely interested in farming;" and that he "was elected to the Fifty-second Congress as a Democrat."[10]

It was reasonable and in every way proper that inasmuch as the Alliance was a national body whose political principles and demands related wholly to national subjects, members of Congress that were also members of the Farmers' Alliance should work together in the national legislature; and the Alliance members from the Northwestern States expected such a union among the members who indorsed the "demands of the Supreme Councils of the National Farmers' Alliance and Industrial Union."[11] But only one

ing that Alliance principles could be achieved working through the Democratic party. By late spring 1892, however, the failure of the Democrats in the House to pass silver legislation or consider a subtreasury bill caused Winn to repudiate his party and join the Populists. He was not renominated in 1892 when the Populists in his district broke into quarrelling factions based on their partisan antecedents. In 1896 the People's party did nominate him for Congress, but he was not elected.

10. For a superb biography of the man who would become the leader of the Southern Populists, see C. Vann Woodward, *Tom Watson: Agrarian Rebel* (New York: Macmillan, 1938).

11. The Supreme Councils of the NFA&IU were the annual meetings of the organization, held in St. Louis in 1889, Ocala in 1890, and Indianapolis in 1891. The Indianapolis meeting had not only reaffirmed the reform

among the Southern members felt it to be his duty to cooperate with the members from the Northwest.

Thomas E. Watson was not a member of the Alliance. He was a Democrat, a lawyer, and "largely interested in farming." In his campaign he had told the farmers of his district that although he was not with them in the flesh, he was with them in the spirit; that he indorsed every one of their principles and demands, and that if he were elected to Congress he would do all that he was able to do in the way of securing legislation along the lines laid down in the Alliance creed. Respecting these statements and pledges as binding obligations on his part, Mr. Watson promptly allied himself with the Northern Independents, and he was agreed upon as their candidate for Speaker.

In the *Congressional Record* for the first session of the Fifty-second Congress, vol. 23, part 1, at page (7) seven, the following entry appears: "Mr. Simpson—I place in nomination for Speaker of the House of Representatives of the Fifty-second Congress the Hon. Thomas E. Watson, a Representative from the state of Georgia." On the next page following (8), Mr. Watson's vote is given: Baker, Clover, Davis, Halvorson, Kem, McKeighan, Otis, Simpson.[12]

demands of the earlier meetings but adopted a resolution instructing Alliance members in the new Congress to avoid any party caucus unless endorsement of Alliance principles were made the test of admission.

12. William Baker was a farmer and stock raiser in Lincoln County, Kansas, and the district lecturer for the Alliance in northwestern Kansas. A former Republican, he was elected to Congress in 1890, 1892, and 1894, the only Kansas Populist to serve three consecutive terms. John Davis of Junction City, Kansas, was a former Grange leader and twice the unsuccessful nominee of the Greenbackers for Congress. A prolific writer for financial and labor reform issues, he was the editor of the *Junction City Tribune*. He was elected to Congress in both 1890 and 1892 before losing in 1894. Kittel Halvorson was a Norwegian immigrant who became a farmer in Minnesota, where he was elected to the state legislature in 1886 and, as the nominee of Populists and Prohibitionists, to Congress in 1890. He was not active in Congress and was not reelected, although he remained of local importance in the People's party. Omer M. Kem, a farmer and Alliance or-

Halvorson was from Minnesota, Kem and McKeighan from Nebraska. The others were all from Kansas.

Charles F. Crisp of Georgia[13] was the Democratic candidate for Speaker, and every Alliance member from the Southern States voted for him.

In the Senate the two Alliance men—Gordon and Irby—were both austerely Democratic in their language and votes. When Mr. Irby was questioned by a Northwestern Senator who had hoped to have the President of the South Carolina State Farmers' Alliance for a co-worker in the Senate, he answered: "Well, sir, we Alliance men in the South are all Democrats." Senator Irby never proposed in the Senate a single measure, bill, amendment, or resolution looking to the incorporation of any Alliance doctrine in the legislation

ganizer from Broken Bow, Nebraska, was elected to Congress as a Populist in 1890, 1892, and 1894. William A. McKeighan was a farmer from Red Cloud, Nebraska, who was twice elected to Congress, 1890 and 1892, with Democratic help through fusion. John Grant Otis of Topeka, Kansas, was a close personal friend of Peffer's. A dairy farmer who was the Kansas state lecturer of the Grange, Otis had earlier left the Republican party for the Greenbackers and Prohibitionists and in 1890 took a major role in organizing the Kansas People's party as well as being elected to Congress on the Populist ticket. He also helped organize the national party and was an earnest advocate of Populist principles in Congress, but he failed of renomination in 1892 because of his hostility to fusion. Thereafter, he was active among the extreme mid-road Populists before finally becoming a socialist. "Sockless Jerry" Simpson of Medicine Lodge, Kansas, was a former Greenbacker who had unsuccessfully run as a Union Labor candidate for the state legislature in 1888. A clever and popular stump speaker, Simpson professed to be a single-taxer, but his views were rather idiosyncratic and strikingly flexible. He was elected to Congress three times with the fusion assistance of Democrats, in 1890, 1892, and 1896.

13. Charles F. Crisp was a lawyer and judge from Ellaville, Georgia, who served in Congress from 1883 until his death in 1896. A conservative Democrat, Crisp rejected the subtreasury and other Alliance reform demands. Twice elected Speaker of the United States House of Representatives, Crisp used his power to frustrate Populist members of Congress and their reform measures.

of the country.[14] The same observation is true in the case of Senator Gordon, and the fact is passing strange, for that gentleman has an acute and manly sense of honor in his mental and moral makeup, and he had publicly hailed the advent of the Alliance and approved its demands before his election.

The Alliance was strict with candidates for office. The farmers would not support a candidate who would not approve the "demands" and promise to support them. Every man seeking a seat in Congress had to sign papers if he was not well known to be grounded in the faith. The first of the "demands," as the reader will remember, was that for the abolition of national banks and the substitution of legal tender Treasury notes in place of the bank notes.

In North Carolina, in some if not all cases, the Alliance presented printed cards to the candidates, the cards reciting all the "demands," with space enough between [each of] them for the candidates' approval and signature. Here is the form:

I approve the above demand, and, if elected to a seat in Congress, will endeavor to have it enacted into law.

14. The conscientious and somewhat abstemious Peffer was appalled by this representative of Southern Democrats. Irby was a violent and drunken man given to tirades and often implicated in scandal. During his six years in the Senate he made only two short speeches, took no action to promote the few bills he introduced, and rarely appeared for roll call votes. One historian has described as no exaggeration the conclusion of a contemporary editor who wrote of Irby's performance: "This is the worst record that can be found against any sound, healthy man who ever sat in the Senate of the United States." See Francis Butler Simkins, *Pitchfork Ben Tillman: South Carolinian* (Baton Rouge: Louisiana State University Press, 1944), 329. Moreover, as Peffer recognized, Irby had no interest in reform at all and was willing to jettison even silver and accept a goldbug Democratic party and force other South Carolina Democrats to do the same. Tillman finally turned against Irby, forcing him to withdraw from a reelection contest in 1896.

This form of card was used in North Carolina in 1890. The signature had to be written in the presence of a witness, who also signed and then forwarded the pledge to headquarters.

Different methods were employed in different places, but everywhere candidates for Congress had to promise to do what they could to procure legislation demanded by the Alliance before they could rely on the support of that body. Members of the order who were well and publicly known to be in earnest sympathy with the objects sought to be accomplished by the farmers were not subjected to this searching ordeal.

In the case of General Gordon the following dispatch, dated Atlanta, Georgia, May 26, 1890, shows that even so eminent and distinguished a man as he had to recognize the men that held the plow.

> Governor John B. Gordon, who is now a candidate to succeed Senator Joseph E. Brown in the Senate, has placed himself in line with the Farmers' Alliance and approved their scheme. In a letter written to the Secretary of the State Alliance today, after reviewing the constitution, he says: "In view of these efforts to secure organization during so many years of my past life, it is scarcely necessary for me to say that I hail the advent of the Farmers' Alliance as the possible final realization of a long cherished hope; nor is it necessary, with my past record before you, to say that I indorse, without reservation and with unabated emphasis, the policy of the Alliance for the increase of the circulating medium of the country."

That dispatch was read in the United States Senate on September 4, 1893, when the matter pending was the bill to repeal the purchasing clause of the Sherman silver act, for which purpose [Democratic] President [Grover] Cleveland had called Congress together in extraordinary session. Senator Gordon advocated the passage of the bill, and his attention being called to the telegram, he said: "If it will not interrupt the Senator from Kansas, I will distinctly say that I indorse now all that I said then; but I do not indorse the Farmers' Alliance since it has fallen from grace." (See *Congressional Record*, vol. 25, part 1, page 1,200.)

An effort was made to get the independent element in Congress together at a meeting in the office of the *National Economist* early in the session which began in December, 1891. The Alliance members from Georgia and Kansas were present, and after a long and at times a heated debate it was evident that the Georgia men, excepting Watson, had no intention of taking any political action outside the Democratic party.

Southern Democrats expected their party to profit by defections in the Republican ranks in the Northwest, where much the larger proportion of Alliance men had belonged to that party. It was common for the Northern independent Representatives to be approached familiarly by stalwart Democrats from Southern territory, as if it were taken as a matter of course that men who had left the Republicans would surely lodge in the party of Buchanan.

It may be said with substantial accuracy that few of the leading Alliance men in any part of the South before 1892 favored separate political action. At the Cincinnati conference, May 1891, Alabama, Florida, Georgia, Louisiana, and North Carolina had only ten delegates in attendance. Arkansas and Tennessee had six each, and Texas had twenty-six.

It was well known and generally understood that the high officials of the Alliance in Southern States were all opposed to the holding of any conference looking toward party organization. They expected to do all their work through the Democracy. That party was supreme in the States of the South, and all the farmers had to do in order to secure favorable party action was to get a majority of the voters there on their side. And it is not at all improbable that they would have succeeded in that particular if the Democratic candidate for the Presidency in 1892 had been friendly to the restoration of silver coinage; for it was not until Mr. Cleveland's nomination seemed certain that Southern Alliance men seriously considered the proposition submitted by the conference at Cincinnati. They knew that Mr. Cleveland was against their demands, and they knew also that whatever of vitality there was in the Cincinnati movement was all on their side. And they knew another thing—that so far as Alliance men were concerned a large majority of them dwelt south of the Ohio River. Cleveland's candidacy impelled them to take chances with the new party.

III
Early Attempts of the Democracy to Get Control of the People's Party— Defeat of the First State Ticket and Election of Mr. Peffer to the Senate

The conference which prepared and issued the call for a [Kansas] State [Populist] convention was composed of ninety delegates, representing five different industrial bodies, as follows:

Farmers' Alliance and Industrial Union	41
Patrons of Husbandry	7
Knights of Labor	28
Farmers' Mutual Benefit Association	10
Single Tax clubs	4
Total	90

The report of the Committee on Order of Business, which was adopted, provided for the appointment of a State Central Committee, to consist of one member of the Farmers' Alliance and Industrial Union for each Congressional district and one member of each of the other organizations represented in the conference whenever those organizations had a membership in the district. John F. Willits of Jefferson County[1] and S. W. Coombs of Topeka were added

1. John F. Willits of McLouth had been a farmer in Jefferson County for twenty years in 1890. He had previously been a Republican, serving in the state legislature in the 1870s, but he had then become a Greenbacker

to the Central Committee, and Willits was made chairman and Coombs secretary.[2] The name of the new political body, it was agreed, should be "People's Party," under which "we will base our political action, and the St. Louis demands shall be considered the

and, later, a member of the Union Labor party. He was the state lecturer of the Kansas Grange from 1877 to 1882 and took an active role in the Farmers' Alliance after its appearance, serving as president of the Jefferson County Farmers' Alliance in 1889, then as president of the state Alliance, twice as national lecturer of the NFA&IU, and finally as national president in 1895–1896. A powerful speaker who refused to compromise his radical beliefs or accept fusion with the unregenerate, Willits necessarily had mixed success as a politician and finally joined the Socialist party, which several times nominated him for Congress after 1900.

2. Peffer is slightly confused here. S. W. Coombs of Topeka was added to the People's State Central Committee as an at-large member, but it was S. W. Chase of Cowley County who was elected secretary. Seth W. "Dick" Chase had bolted the Cowley County Republican party in 1889 and with Benjamin H. Clover had helped organize a "People's ticket" in that year's local elections. Willits had organized a similar local third party in Jefferson County in 1889, and these were in some respects the forerunners to the state-level third party that Willits, Clover, and Chase were instrumental in launching in 1890. When Willits was nominated for governor in August, Chase became the chair of the state committee. Chase's somewhat autocratic methods ultimately provoked such dissatisfaction that in early 1891 Peffer was importuned to call a meeting of the Populist committee (the committee held its meetings in the offices of Peffer's *Kansas Farmer* in Topeka), and Chase was replaced by Levi "Dave" Dumbauld of Lyon County. In 1893 Chase was appointed by Populist Governor Lorenzo D. Lewelling as warden of the state penitentiary, where he became embroiled in charges of misconduct that spilled over into a major political issue in 1894. He was removed from that position in 1895. S. W. Coombs played no such major role as did Chase, but was again a member of the Populist State Central Committee in 1892. An opponent of fusion, Coombs complained that the committee under Dumbauld favored fusion and would not even notify the antifusion members of committee meetings. (See *Washington Post*, May 27, 1892.) In 1894, Coombs (then of Riley County) was an antifusion delegate to the Populist state convention and opposed the renomination of Lewelling and the other Populist state officeholders. (See *Topeka Daily Capital*, June 12, 1894.)

basis of the political principles of the organization." The St. Louis demands were published with the proceedings of the conference.

Among the [additional] resolutions adopted was this one:

> "That we will not support for office any member of our organization who will accept a nomination from either of the old parties, but will consider such member a traitor to our cause."

And this one:

> "That we demand that all honorably discharged soldiers, their widows and orphans be pensioned, and that all pledges made to them be complied with as fully as in the case of the bondholder."

That conference took place on June 12, 1890. On or about the 18th day of July, the State Central Committee issued an address to its constituents, from which the following two passages are taken:

> We are not contending for the emoluments of office, for we have a higher and nobler ambition. We are contending for the great principles of equality, the basic principles of the republic, to which our fathers dedicated their lives, their fortunes, and their sacred honor. May God's providence direct the coming contest, may we lay aside selfishness and petty jealousies, and all unite at the ballot-box and save the nation from the curse that has blotted out all the ancient civilizations of the world.
>
> We have taken upon ourselves non-partisan political action. We have done the best we could for the people, as God gives us to see it. We have votes enough within our consolidated order to carry the State, and we ask you to stand nobly by the action of your delegates here today. We ask you to nominate true men to the various offices and sustain them

with your votes on election day. It matters not what party they have been identified with heretofore. We all come from some party; we want true men, regardless of party, in whom we can have confidence.

About a week before the address was issued the following notice and request was sent out by the State Central Committee:

To the Members of the Different Organizations Comprising the People's Party of Kansas, Greeting:

We, your committee, have made arrangements with the publishers of the *Advocate* and *Kansas Farmer* for a trial subscription price of 25 cents for four months to each paper, in clubs of ten or more. This will enable us to keep before you the complete campaign work in an official form; all the attacks made on our party by the partisan press will be answered, and you will be kept thoroughly posted on every movement. We feel that this is by far the best means to fight our battle and to win our glorious cause. Now, brethren, do not miss this chance to furnish your members with a means that will enable them to vote intelligently.

The *Advocate* was a new paper, started by Dr. S. McLallin, a courageous, intelligent, and conscientious man.[3] The paper was devoted wholly to the work of the Farmers' Alliance and kindred bodies. The *Kansas Farmer* was devoting one or two pages every week to Alliance matter.

3. Stephen McLallin, in the words of the Populist writer Annie L. Diggs, was "a compound of a Greek philosopher, of the austere, undemonstrative Scotchman, and the modern socialist" (quoted in O. Gene Clanton, *Kansas Populism: Ideas and Men* [Lawrence: University Press of Kansas, 1969], 53). After a career as a physician, McLallin had turned to journalism and in 1889 launched the *Advocate* in Meriden, Jefferson County, before relocating it to Topeka in 1890. Committed to the organiza-

There were three other papers in Kansas at the time that were supporting this new movement—namely: the *Junction City Tribune*, owned and edited by John Davis, once a friend and acquaintance of Abraham Lincoln and one of the original Greenbackers; the *Ottawa Journal*, E. H. Snow's paper, likewise a Greenbacker; and the *American Non-Conformist* at Winfield, conducted by the Vincent brothers.[4] These three papers had been actively supporting the Union Labor party, which was merged in the new movement.

tion of a third party well before Peffer's *Kansas Farmer*, the *Advocate* under McLallin was instrumental in spreading the gospel of Populism and by the mid 1890s was easily the most important Populist newspaper in America. McLallin was active in Populist politics, being elected a delegate to the 1892 Omaha Convention, for example, but he primarily served the cause through his invariably astute editorials. McLallin's death in 1896 deprived the Populists of one of their strongest voices against fusion and silver politics.

4. While the five newspapers named here were the most important journals supporting the new People's party, there were in fact many other newspapers, perhaps two hundred or more, that championed the movement. The prominence of Edwin H. Snow, editor of the *Ottawa Journal and Triumph*, was demonstrated when the Populist-controlled state legislature elected him as state printer in 1891. Henry, Cuthbert, and Leopold Vincent, editors of the *American Nonconformist and Kansas Industrial Liberator*, published in Winfield from 1886 to 1891, were even more influential, not only in Kansas but nationally as well. Committed to what they called "the most ultra reform" principles, the Vincents had been Greenbackers and Union Laborites and took a crucial role in establishing Populism in America. Cuthbert Vincent became one of the national directors of the National Reform Press Association, following its formation at the 1890 Ocala meeting, and in September 1891, the Vincents moved the *Nonconformist* to Indianapolis to better advocate Populist principles on the national level. Henry soon moved on to Chicago and launched the *Searchlight* as a radical labor and Populist paper. More radical than Peffer (or nearly any other Populist), the Vincents had constantly prodded and pushed him in 1889–1890 to break from the Republicans and then opposed his election to the Senate in 1891 as "a very mediocre type of reform" (*American Nonconformist*, January 15, 1891). Nevertheless, they came to respect Peffer, hired his son Elwood as an editor in Indianapolis, and

The call for a convention having settled the question whether political action was to be taken, Democrat politicians at once set to work on a scheme to get control of the movement by securing the nomination of a Democrat as the People's party candidate for Governor. There were 115 different Alliances in the State, and as they numbered over 100,000 voters, many more than all the other orders in the union combined, the Alliance people quite naturally felt disposed to put the President of the State Alliance, B. H. Clover, at the head of the State ticket. President Clover listened to the suggestion and, while not openly approving it, modestly said he had doubts about his fitness for so responsible a position. He had never had any experience in public affairs, he said, and this he urged as an objection. It was suggested to him that the office of Governor is executive purely; that the Governor's duty is not to make laws but, as the State constitution provides, to "see that the laws are faithfully executed."

In the latter part of July Mr. Clover, in a public letter without date, declined to permit his name to go before the convention. "I have no ambition for office," he said in his letter; "if I had, this is surely an opportunity of which I should be proud. I cannot suffer myself to be put in the light of a designing man and a seeker after office by reason of the prominent part I have taken in the Alliance work." The letter concluded with these words: "Brothers and friends, for the sake of our homes, our families, and our cause, make no mistake."

The letter was published on the 30th of July, just two weeks before the day appointed for the convention. A few days afterwards the editor of the *Kansas Farmer* was approached by a well-known Democrat, who proposed the name of ex-Governor Charles Robin-

---

joined him in consistently opposing the diminution of Omaha Populism to silver politics. For their Kansas career, see Harold Piehler, "Henry Vincent: Kansas Populist and Radical-Reform Journalist," *Kansas History* 2 (Spring 1979): 14–25.

son,[5] a Democrat, as a suitable person to head the People's Party State ticket, and among the reasons for this move it was averred that by placing Governor Robinson at the head of the new party, if successful, it would be an easy matter and the proper and logical thing to do to send the *Kansas Farmer* editor to the United States Senate as the successor of Mr. Ingalls. The interviewing Democrat was promptly informed, first, that Charles Robinson would not be named for Governor by the People's Party convention, and, second, that the editor of the *Kansas Farmer* was not a candidate for the Senate.

A few days later the editor aforesaid and Mr. Clover met on a railway train, and, in conversation about the coming convention, Mr. Clover inquired what course the *Kansas Farmer* would take in the event of Robinson's nomination for Governor on the People's ticket. Mr. Clover was informed that it was useless to consider the subject of his question, for the reason that such nomination would not be made. Mr. Clover argued quite earnestly in Robinson's favor, but received in reply only, "Robinson will not be nominated."

Ex-Governor Robinson was a man of great force of character—honest, aggressive, and fearless. He was the first Governor of the State, and that alone discloses his political affiliations at that time. When Kansas adopted a prohibitory liquor amendment to her constitution, Governor Robinson took a bold and violent stand against it and the laws passed for its enforcement. He went so far as to publicly advise Judges, jurors, Sheriffs, and the people individually to defy the law. The Republican party at once made the amendment

5. Charles Robinson of Lawrence was one of the state's most notable citizens. He had been both the free-state governor of Territorial Kansas in the 1850s and the first governor of the new state in the early 1860s. He was a founder of the University of Kansas and a successful farmer and landowner who held state offices in the Grange. A financial and tariff reformer, he had also been the Greenback candidate for governor in 1882 and a Democratic candidate for Congress in 1886. For a sympathetic biography, see Don W. Wilson, *Governor Charles Robinson of Kansas* (Lawrence: University Press of Kansas, 1975).

and its enforcement part of the party creed. Robinson acted with the Democratic party, which denounced prohibition and demanded a resubmission of the amendment to a popular vote. He had offended all Prohibitionists by the bitterness of his attacks, and he had once been a candidate for Congress in 1886 on the Democratic ticket.

In the *Kansas Farmer* of August 6, 1890, just one week before convention day, the following article appeared as an editorial:

WHO FOR GOVERNOR?—Since the publication of Mr. Clover's letter refusing to permit the use of his name as a candidate for Governor, members of the People's party are much at sea in relation to that particular matter. The feeling in his favor was practically unanimous, and, though he never encouraged those who mentioned the subject to him, it was not generally believed that he would decline a nomination if it were tendered.

Now, what is to be done? A better way of putting the question is, What ought to be done? In the first place, let us consider a moment what ought not to be done. No man ought to be placed at the head of the ticket who has been so long and publicly identified with any particular social, political, or religious movement as to have become, on that account, obnoxious to large classes of the people. The man with a repulsive hobby ought not to be nominated. Nor should any person whose name would suggest particular policies that are not popular with a majority of the people, and who, for that reason, would pass as the platform in place of the platform itself. These things are breakers, and they must be avoided. And as to what ought to be done, let us think a moment. This movement is of the people—the masses of workers; therefore, the man who heads the ticket ought to be, first of all, a worker, one who earns his livelihood by his own labor.

A large majority of persons enlisted in the people's movement are temperance people—most of them outspoken prohibitionists. Ninety per cent of Kansas farmers are opposed to dramshops in any form, and Knights of Labor will not take into their order a man or woman who is in any way interested in the liquor traffic; therefore, the People's candidate ought to be on the people's side of the liquor question.

A large proportion of the people in this movement were soldiers in the Union army, and the People's party will have to do some work along the soldier's line, and that suggests that the first name on the ticket should be that of a man who can show an honorable discharge from the military service in the war of the slaveholders' rebellion.

A large majority of persons who expect to vote the People's ticket this year are Republicans, and for that reason one of that class ought to head the ticket.

It will not be difficult to find a man with all these qualifications and not subject to any of the objections first above mentioned. With such a candidate at the head of the ticket, the other places distributed fairly among the different classes of voters who are joined in the movement, there is good reason to expect success; for, in that case, we would not only be stronger among ourselves, but we would draw largely from other sources. Wisdom in this matter will serve as well all through the fight; while a mistake now may be equivalent to cutting off half our forces.[6]

6. Robinson, who had been actively seeking the Populist nomination, was furious with this editorial, the purpose of which seemed clear to him. Writing to a supporter, W. H. T. Wakefield of Lawrence, the 1888 vice-presidential nominee of the Union Labor party, Robinson complained, "You can see that I am a most complete outcast from the People's party, according to Mr. Peffer, and I do not want to disturb him in his conviction-less fight, led by a prohibition republican who never entertained a conviction unless it was first found to be popular" (quoted in *Topeka Democrat*, August 14, 1890). Other observers believed that the editorial was designed to eliminate Robinson in place of Peffer himself. The *Kansas City Journal* concluded that "Peffer stands forth as the only man who can fill the bill" (quoted in *Topeka Daily Capital*, August 10, 1890). Interestingly, Republi-

The convention was held on the 13th day of August, with 521 delegates present, of whom about 200 were ex-union soldiers, nearly all of whom had been Republicans. The platform, after recognizing "Almighty God as the rightful sovereign of nations," and reciting the fact that the convention was "composed of members from all shades of political belief," set forth the following as "the great underlying principles of the questions aforesaid and exemplified in the St. Louis demands":

> Labor is the beginning of progress, the foundation of wealth, and the laborer is entitled to a good living and a fair share of the profits which result from his labor.
>
> The use of labor saving machinery should shorten the hours of toil and inure to the benefit of the employed equally with the employer.
>
> The earth is the common heritage of the people; every person born into the world is entitled equally with all others to a place to live and earn a living, and any system of government that does not maintain and protect this inalienable right is wrong and should be changed or abolished.

Then follows a statement favoring service pension; after that the St. Louis demands with a few others opposing "usurious interest," asking a "reasonable stay of execution in all cases of foreclosures of mortgages on real estate, and a reasonable extension of time before the confirmation of Sheriff sales"; opposition to "trusts and combines," favoring adjustment of salaries of public officers, ask-

---

can leader Senator Preston B. Plumb concurred with Peffer's reasoning and thought Robinson a weak candidate. He wrote privately to the editor of the *Topeka Capital* that Robinson "is a good man, but is so bound to quarrel with everybody that he turns myriads of people against him who would otherwise be his friends." Plumb to J. K. Hudson, September 11, 1890, J. K. Hudson Papers, KSHS.

ing the adoption of the Australian ballot system, and urging the "Crawford system of primaries."[7]

The friends of Governor Robinson presented his name to the convention for nomination as a candidate for Governor, and he was beaten three to one by John F. Willits, a farmer, an ex-union soldier, a prohibitionist, and a former Republican, who had not made himself obnoxious by too much talking on any subject.

Had Mr. Robinson succeeded in the effort to secure the People's nomination for Governor there would not have been any Democratic State ticket put out that year, but failing in that direction to capture the new party, a Democratic convention was called to meet at Wichita on September 19, for the purpose of nominating Democratic candidates for all the State offices, and Charles Robinson headed the ticket named at that place and time.

The vote on Governor at the election, November, was as follows:

Republican (Humphrey)	115,025
Populist (Willits)	106,972
Democrat (Robinson)	71,357
Prohibition (Richardson)	1,240

The Republican and Populist candidates for Governor ran behind their associates on their respective tickets, while Robinson ran ahead. Following is the vote on Lieutenant Governor:

7. The making of party nominations by direct vote of party members rather than indirectly by delegate conventions had been initiated by local Democrats in Crawford County, Pennsylvania, in 1842. Thereafter, this "Crawford system" of democratic nominations was nearly always ignored by the major parties, but radical third parties, like the Populists, sometimes adopted it voluntarily, at least in scattered locations, and called for its wider implementation. Beginning in the early twentieth century, states began to mandate such direct primaries.

Republican (Felt)	120,468
Populist (Shinn)	115,553
Democrat (Banta)	57,021

In order to learn where the votes of the new party came from, let us look at the returns of the last preceding State election—1888—for Presidential Electors:

Republican	182,904
Democrat	102,745
Union Labor	37,788
Prohibition	6,700
Total	330,137

Now, compare the vote of the two years:

THE VOTE

PARTY	1888	1890	Loss.	Gain.
Republican	182,904	120,969	61,935	.....
People's	.....	115,933	.....	115,933
Democratic	102,745	71,357	31,388	.....
Union Labor	37,788	.....	37,788	.....
Prohibition	6,700	1,316	5,384	.....
Totals	330,137	309,575	136,495	115,933

A fair comparison of these figures gives us the following estimate[8] of the antecedents of the voters that made the 115,000 Populists in 1890:

8. In 1890, Peffer made a slightly different estimate, suggesting proportionately fewer Republicans (45,000), Union Laborites (33,000), and Prohi

Former Republicans	48,000
Former Democrats	25,000
Former Union Labor	37,000
Former Prohibition	5,000
Total	115,000

The Union Labor people had nearly all been Republicans. Let it be added here, lest it be forgotten, that B. H. Clover, President of the Kansas State Farmers' Alliance and Industrial Union, who refused to let his name be used before the nominating convention as a candidate for Governor on the ground that his position would not justify him in seeking office, and who, after such refusal, urged the nomination of ex-Governor Robinson, a Democrat, soon became a candidate for Congress in the Third Congressional District of Kansas, received Democratic support, and was elected by nearly 4,000 majority over his Republican competitor.

The politics of the members of the Legislature chosen at the same election was as follows: Populists, 96; Republicans, 24; Democrats, 5. Of the 96 Populists, 83 had voted the Republican ticket in 1888; the other 13 had voted the Union Labor ticket, and all of them had once been Republicans. Of these 83 Populist members who had been Republicans 41 had served their country as soldiers in the Union army.

The vote for United States Senator in the two Houses of the Legislature separately, January 27, 1891, shows that the one Democrat in the Senate, and the five Democrats in the House, all voted for a member of their own party for Senator. In the joint convention of the two Houses next day the Democrat Senator and two of his

bitionists (2,000), and a larger number of former Democrats (35,000). See William A. Peffer, *The Farmer's Side: His Troubles and Their Remedy* (New York: Appleton, 1891), 157.

VOL. 20 NO. 497   APRIL 25 1891   PRICE 10 CENTS

Judge

ENTERED AT THE POST OFFICE AT NEW YORK AS SECOND-CLASS MATTER.   COPYRIGHT 1891 BY THE JUDGE PUBLISHING CO.

A MIGHTY POOR EXCHANGE.
From the sublime to the ridiculous.

*A Republican effort to belittle the elections of Peffer to the Senate and fellow Kansas Populist "Sockless Jerry" Simpson to the House by comparing the caricatured newcomers to the departing Republican congressional leaders Senator George Edmunds of Vermont and Congressman William McKinley of Ohio. (*Judge, *April 25, 1891)* party colleagues in the House again voted for their own party man. The other three Democrats in the House voted for the Populist nominee, [William A. Peffer,] whose majority without these three votes would have been thirty-five.

IV
Beginning of the Fusion Movement

That the Democratic party had no sympathy with the principles and doctrines of the Populists at the beginning of that movement needs no proof. It was obvious—self-evident. In the Southern States the antagonism was not only clearly manifest—it was deepseated and to the extent of actual physical fighting. Populism was not in accord with Democracy on any essential point, and the lines of difference were distinctly drawn. In 1892, in all the larger matters, Populism and Democracy were at war. One of the good results expected to come from the rise of the new party in the Southern States was that it would break the solid South, and it was the fear and dread of such an ending that impelled the Democrats there to oppose the Populist movement. It was the political action of the Farmers' Alliance that General and Senator Gordon had in mind when he said the organization had fallen from grace.

The Southern Alliance people were slow and hesitating about seeking redress of grievances through separate political action until they became satisfied that Grover Cleveland probably would be the Democracy's candidate for the Presidency in 1892. Alabama, that year, gave 85,181 votes for Weaver to 131,138 for Cleveland and 9,197 for [Republican Benjamin] Harrison. Georgia gave 42,937 votes for Weaver to 129,361 for Cleveland and 48,305 for Harrison. Texas' vote was: Weaver, 99,688; Cleveland, 239,148; Harrison, 77,478. It is thus seen that in the South party lines were as clearly drawn in 1892 as they were in Kansas two years before. Fusion did not begin among the Southern Populists nor in the States of the South. Kansas is the birthplace of this poisonous political drug.

As was shown in the last preceding one of these articles, the attempt to force a Democrat on the head of the Populist State ticket in 1890 was not successful, but in the election of Congressmen Democratic influence was more powerful. While Mr. Clover did not officially recognize the assistance of Democratic voters he did in fact receive it; and while there is nothing on record other than a few pregnant facts to support the belief, it was then, as it is now, believed that Mr. Clover's election to Congress was aided by Democrats in consideration of his declining a nomination for Governor and thus making room for Robinson, the Democrat.

There were then, as there are now, seven Congressional districts in the State. In four of them—the First, Second, Fifth, and Sixth—there were candidates for each and all parties; but in the Third, Fourth, and Seventh Districts the Democrats had no candidates. The Third was Clover's district. In the *Congressional Directory* for the first session of the Fifty-second Congress, at page 40 it is recorded of Mr. Clover that he "was elected to the Fifty-second Congress as a candidate of the Farmers' Alliance."On the same page of the same document it appears that Mr. Otis of the Fourth District "was elected . . . as People's party candidate." In the Fifth District Sidney G. Cooke[1] had been nominated by the Democrats, but was persuaded to withdraw. On the next page, 41, of the same book it appears that Jerry Simpson of the Seventh District "was nominated for Congress by the People's party and elected by the aid of the Democrats, who indorsed his nomination, receiving 32,603 votes, against 25,181 votes for James R. Hallowell,[2] Republican, and 9 votes scattering."

1. Sidney G. Cooke of Herington, Kansas, was a conservative banker and lawyer who vigorously opposed Populism. Although he frequently denounced fusion between Democrats and Populists, he sometimes promoted it, as in this instance.
2. James R. Hallowell of Wichita was one of the state's most able and

In Jerry Simpson's district, in 1890, in the same State, same year, and same campaign, where and when the Populist party had its origin, was the first successful effort to unite the Populists and Democrats.

In Illinois and South Dakota during the sessions of the Legislatures of those States in 1891 there was a good deal of difficulty in making [the] choice of a United States Senator. In the Illinois case three members of the Legislature belonged to the Farmers' Mutual Benefit Association, and the two great parties in joint convention of the Legislature were so evenly divided that these three farmers held the balance of power, and they were voting for their own candidate for Senator, Mr. Streeter.[3]

General John M. Palmer[4] was the candidate of the Democrats, and his supporters much desired the assistance of the F.M.B.A.

prominent Republicans. He had been a Civil War hero, a state senator (from Cherokee County), the United States District Attorney for Kansas, and an influential delegate to the Republican National Conventions in both 1884 and 1888. He had even been "elected" congressman-at-large when state leaders argued that its exploding population entitled Kansas to another representative, but of course the Democratic House of Representatives refused to seat him. Hallowell was also regarded by the leading Republican newspaper as "one of the best political stump speakers in the state" (*Topeka Daily Capital*, August 1, 1890). The Republicans sought to exploit these abilities by arranging a debate between their "Prince Hal" and the unpolished Jerry Simpson. Simpson, of course, devastated Hallowell and in doing so earned his own nickname, "Sockless Jerry."

3. Alson J. Streeter of New Windsor, Illinois, was a former Granger, Greenbacker, president of the National ("Northern") Farmers' Alliance, and the presidential nominee of the Union Labor party in 1888.

4. John M. Palmer, a Union Army general during the Civil War and a former governor of Illinois, was a prominent corporate attorney. Elected to the United States Senate in 1891, he thereafter pursued an increasingly conservative course, not only opposing silver legislation, as Peffer indicates below, but bolting the Democratic nomination of William Jennings Bryan in 1896 to run as the presidential nominee of the Gold Democrats.

men. Jerry Simpson, recently elected to Congress in the Seventh District of Kansas, "by the aid of the Democrats, who indorsed his nomination," went to Springfield and rendered what assistance he could in securing the election of General Palmer. A conference between the General and the three Streeter men was arranged, and it resulted in securing the votes of two of the three—enough to elect Palmer on the 154th ballot. Among the arguments submitted to the F.M.B.A. members were two of leading importance: one was that in case of Palmer's election by the aid of these men's votes the Democratic members of the South Dakota Legislature would vote for James H. Kyle, a member of the State Senate at the time and an Independent.[5] The other argument was that in the case of General Palmer's election to the Senate he would be classed among the friends of silver.

Populists were led to believe that General Palmer's election was at least a partial victory for them, and the deception was not discovered until, when Senator Palmer's attention was called to that fact by the Populist Senator from Kansas during the silver debate in the Senate in 1893, he, Palmer, denied that he ever had entered into any such agreement or made or authorized any such a pledge. He stated in open Senate that during the entire time of the conference a stenographer was present taking down all that was said, and he offered to show an official copy of the interview to the Senator from Kansas at any time he might wish to look it over.

5. James H. Kyle was a minister from Aberdeen, South Dakota. The South Dakota Independents (that is, Populists) elected him in 1890 to the state senate and, with Democratic assistance, in 1891 to the United States Senate. In 1897 he was reelected by Republican votes over the opposition of the Populists, an indication of the relatively conservative and expedient career he pursued. Indeed, his behavior in Congress once prompted other Populist senators to deny he was a Populist at all. For an account of the maneuvering over the election of Palmer in Illinois and Kyle in South Dakota, which stresses its destructive consequences for third party action, see Roy V. Scott, *The Agrarian Movement in Illinois, 1880–1896* (Urbana: University of Illinois Press, 1962), 103–115.

In 1892 while Populists in the Southern States were fighting the Democracy, in Kansas a complete and successful fusion of the two parties was effected. The Democrats did not put out a State ticket in Kansas that year. They met in regular party convention, and, after a long, serious, and acrimonious debate, it was determined to preserve the party organization, publish a party platform, and then support the Populist ticket from top to bottom. Of course this sacrifice was not accidental. On the contrary, it was deliberately planned and quite carefully executed, not for the benefit of Populism, but for advantages to accrue the Democratic party, as the sequel will show.

The census of 1890 disclosed the fact that Kansas was entitled to one additional Congressman, but the Legislature not having redistricted the State, the eighth Congressman was assigned to the State-at-large, and Colonel W. A. Harris,[6] once a Confederate soldier, was nominated by the State Populist convention for Congressman-at-large. Colonel Harris was indorsed by the Democratic State convention.

In the First, Fifth, and Sixth Districts there were [only nominal] Democratic candidates, and they received 161 votes in the First, 508 in the Fifth (although the candidate had withdrawn), and 1,301 in the Sixth, respectively. In the Third District T. J. Hudson,[7] the Populist nominee, was indorsed by the Democrats.

6. William A. Harris of Linwood, Kansas, was a native Virginian and former Democrat who was a well-to-do stockraiser and leader of the Leavenworth County Farmers' Alliance. Harris opposed many of the basic Populist economic demands, such as the subtreasury, debtor relief, and paper money, and only belatedly joined the People's party. He always maintained close ties with the Democrats and consistently promoted Populist-Democratic fusion, which helped elect him, in turn, to Congress in 1892, the Kansas state senate in 1896, and the United States Senate in 1897. He then returned openly to the Democratic party and was the Democratic nominee for governor in 1906.

7. Thomas Jefferson Hudson was a prominent lawyer from Fredonia, Kansas, where in the 1870s he had been a neighbor and friend of Peffer

S. S. King [of Kansas City], a lawyer of ability, a pleasing speaker, a good campaigner, and who, with his little book, "Bond-holders and Breadwinners," and his explanatory charts, did effective service in the State campaign two years before, was nominated in 1892 by the Populists of the second District as their candidate for Congress. Much against the wishes of his political and personal friends near him, he was prevailed upon, after he had begun his canvass, to withdraw in favor of Colonel H. L. Moore, a Democrat.[8] This withdrawal of King was not without promise and hope of reward in the event of the success of the Populist State ticket; and it may as well be stated here that the State ticket was successful, that Mr. King claimed and demanded a fulfillment of the promise made to him, and was disappointed.

In the Fourth District, John G. Otis, as clean and honest a man as lived in the State, who, two years before, had been elected as the people's candidate, and who, in accord with the unwritten law of politics, was entitled to a second nomination, was brushed aside for Dr. E. V. Wharton[9] in order to please the Democrats.

when the latter had been city attorney and editor of the *Fredonia Journal* and Hudson had been the town's mayor. Hudson had also been a state legislator from Wilson County in the 1870s and a delegate to the Democratic National Conventions of 1880, 1884, and 1888 before joining the People's party in 1892. He was elected to Congress in 1892 but did not seek reelection in 1894.

8. Horace L. Moore of Lawrence was a prominent merchant and banker who helped organize the Lawrence National Bank, which he later served as a director and vice-president. A Democrat, he had previously been elected treasurer of Douglas County. He successfully contested the apparent election of his Republican opponent in 1892 and was finally seated in Congress as a Democrat in 1894, shortly before being defeated for reelection.

9. Eugene V. Wharton of Yates Center was a physician, the founder of the *Woodson Democrat*, and a former Democratic state legislator. He helped organize the Union Labor party in Woodson County in 1888 and then became a Populist in 1890. Following his 1892 congressional nomination by the Populists, he received a fusion nomination from the Democrats, but he was defeated in the election.

Summarizing the Congressional campaign in Kansas in 1892, the Democrats had a clear field for a candidate of their own party in the Second District, a candidate that they indorsed in the Third and Seventh Districts and for the State-at-large, all of whom were elected in November.

This political bartering extended even to the verge of wrecking the newspaper organ of the party—the *Advocate*. That paper, as before stated, was started about the close of the year 1889 for the sole purpose of aiding and representing the Alliance movement. Early in 1890, in order to introduce the new paper to members of the order, an edition of 65,000 copies was ordered by the officers of the State Alliance and paid for out of the general fund in the treasury. The paper was sent to the county alliances throughout the State for distribution among the members. The *Advocate* and the *Kansas Farmer* were used by the People's Party State Central Committee in the campaign of 1890 as mediums for official communication with local committees and the voters.

After the election in '90 the *Advocate* was recognized as the representative paper of the Populist party in Kansas. Its editor, Dr. McLallin, was a good writer, a clear-headed and aggressive man, in earnest, sincere, and zealous sympathy with this new political departure. He had been a Republican, and, like the rest, he parted with his old associates regretfully and only because his belief that it was his duty to do so was an overpowering force with him.

The next year (1891) a new paper—the *Tribune*—was started at Topeka to advocate the cause of the People's party, but the managers soon discovered that the field was not large enough nor the harvest ripe enough to warrant two Populist papers there, and an effort was made to get the *Tribune* and the *Advocate* together. The new Congressmen and Senator were appealed to for assistance. Senator Peffer gave $1,000 cash. Congressmen Simpson and Otis each gave $200, and Baker $100. Colonel Harris, afterward elected Congressman-at-large, gave $200. Many persons not in office nor desiring to be subscribed smaller amounts—$25 down to $5. The Advocate Publishing Company was incorporated early in 1892 with an authorized capital of $10,000, Dr. McLallin as editor. The *Tribune* was absorbed in the *Advocate*.

The fusion fever getting hold of the party leaders, a movement was begun in the early summer to get a Democratic daily paper in Topeka—one that would support the fusion scheme—and it proved successful. The *Daily Press*, Mr. J. B. Chapman, editor, was moved from Fort Scott and set going at the State capital—a Democratic paper advocating Democratic doctrines and, following the decision of the Democratic State convention, urging on the fusion program. What promise, bargain, or trade, if any, was made as the inducement for this newspaper plan is of course conjectural, for the published evidence is circumstantial.

The *Press* advocated the election of the Populist ticket all the way through; that ticket was successful beyond controversy or doubt, and the state Executive Council, composed of the newly elected Populist State officers, promised the official State printing, which was worth $2,000 or $3,000 a year gross, to the *Daily Press*, the above-mentioned Democratic paper brought to Topeka for the purpose of aiding the Demo-Populist coalition.

But the *Press* did not get the official State printing. The man who was then business manager of the Advocate Publishing Company—Mr. H. A. Heath,[10] a bright and capable man—made it plain to the new Governor and other members of the council that as a politico-commercial arrangement the *Daily Press* scheme was all well enough during the campaign, as such things go; it was politics then, but it was business now; and as the *Advocate*, the recognized organ of the People's party, had neither been informed nor consulted about the matter, it would not be politically safe or even

---

10. H. A. Heath of Topeka was Peffer's close friend and supporter. Previously he had been the major stockholder of the *Kansas Farmer* and, in 1890, decisively backed Peffer's editorial course when other stockholders, including former Republican Governor Samuel J. Crawford, threatened to fire him unless he devoted his attention to "more crops and less politics" (Topeka *Advocate*, August 6, 1890; *Topeka Daily Capital*, August 10, 1890).

comfortable at that time to turn the newspaper patronage of the Populist administration over to the Democratic party. The *Advocate* got the State printing, and the little profit derived from that source kept the paper going during the two years of the Lewelling term, but it never paid expenses afterward, and finally had to be sold, as the sequel will show.

[Senatorial Election of John Martin]

Preston B. Plumb,[11] whose term as United States Senator from Kansas began on March 4, 1889, having died in December, 1891, it became the duty of the Legislature chosen in 1892 to elect a Senator to fill out the remainder of the unexpired term. The makeup of the House of Representatives was in dispute, but the number of Democrats in it could have been counted on the fingers of one hand with one finger out of sight, and, although there was a Populist who, because of his excellent character as a man, because of his ability, and because of his faithful and efficient services in the campaigns of 1890 and 1892, deserved, and in decency ought to have received without a moment's hesitation or debate, the willing and ready vote of every Populist in the body, when the roll was called in joint convention for Senator, John Martin,[12] a lifelong and radical

11. Preston B. Plumb of Emporia was a lawyer, railroad promoter, and bank director and yet, unlike Ingalls, he was very popular among Kansas farmers, whose interests he promoted during his Senatorial career from 1877 through 1891. Although a Republican, he had distinguished himself by voting against the McKinley Tariff as well as by pushing for free silver and other reforms.

12. John Martin of Topeka was a prominent lawyer and former judge and perhaps the leading Kansas Democrat, having been his party's unsuccessful candidate for governor, Congress, and the Senate. His somewhat liberal leanings brought him the support of some Populists for their party's nomination for state supreme court justice in both 1890 and 1892. In the

Democrat, received the vote of each and every Populist present, and he was declared elected.[13]

In his personal sketch at page 42 of the *Congressional Directory* for the third session of the Fifty-third Congress Senator Martin describes the part he took in the campaign of 1892. He says he "was principally instrumental in securing the indorsement by the Democratic State convention of 1892 of the Populist ticket and in bringing about Congressional and county fusion for the purpose of taking the Electoral vote from the Republicans and in securing the Legislature, which plan succeeded."

latter year he actively promoted fusion between Democrats and Populists, thereby incurring the opposition of both radical Populists and conservative Democrats. Sedgwick County Democrats, for instance, denounced him as a "so-called Democratic leader with Populist tendencies" and condemned "the machinations . . . and smooth, oily, and deceptive utterances" by which he secured fusion (quoted in *Kansas Commoner* [Wichita], July 13, 1893). Following his election to the Senate in 1893, he took a prominent role among the Silver Democrats who repudiated Grover Cleveland's conservatism, but he always remained committed to the Democratic party itself.

13. The unanimity of Populist support for Martin was misleading, for it reflected only the discipline of a caucus decision; the party, in fact, was split badly. Lewelling, Simpson, and other fusionist Populists did support Martin as a reward for his fusionist assistance among the Democrats, but many other Populists naturally opposed electing a Democrat, and Frank Doster was the favorite of most of these antifusion legislators. The decisive factor ultimately involved what Peffer here obliquely refers to as the disputed nature of the House of Representatives. Populists had a clear majority in the state senate, but both Republicans and Populists claimed control of the House, and each party organized its own legislative body. The resulting "legislative war" witnessed competing groups of soldiers and armed "deputies" confronting one another on the capitol grounds and growing public anxiety. Fearful that the Democratic majority in the United States Senate would refuse to seat a Populist elected in these circumstances, a majority of the Populist caucus reluctantly agreed to support Martin, whose party standing would guarantee Senate acceptance regardless of the ultimate legal resolution of the legislative dispute. For the legislative war itself, see William E. Parrish, "The Great Kansas Legislative Imbroglio of 1893," *Journal of the West* 7 (October 1968): 471–490.

There is not a word to be said against John Martin as a man, a citizen, and a neighbor. He has many warm personal friends all over Kansas. That he is a trained and skillful politician and that he is aware of that fact is made clear in the above extract showing what part he played in the campaign of 1892.

But Judge Martin never pleaded the Populist cause, he never believed Populist doctrine, he never was of [the] opinion that Populism ought to succeed, and, like an honest man as he is, he never said anything in favor of the success of Populist ideas. He had always been a Democrat of the strictest sect, and that he was among the foremost of his kind in Kansas is proved by his conceded power and influence in his party councils.

It is not because he was not qualified intellectually and morally to fill the office of Senator that his election was out of order, but it was because (1) he belonged to a party whose principles were in direct antagonism to everything which Populists considered fundamental and vital; and (2) because there was at least one man among the Kansas Populists of commanding ability, of great learning, and of deep-seated convictions in harmony with Populist ideas, and who had spent time, and money, and thought, and labor not to defeat Republicans and elect men like Grover Cleveland to office, but to urge reform forward.

Frank Doster[14] never was a Democrat, he never had given aid and comfort to the Democratic party; on the contrary he had begun his

14. Frank Doster of Marion, Kansas, was an unorthodox and radical intellectual who was nevertheless the foremost jurist in the state. A former Republican who was the Greenback nominee for attorney general in 1878, he later joined the Union Labor party and then embraced the People's party. His famous statement in 1891 that "the rights of the user are paramount to the rights of the owner of capital" made him a popular figure among Populists and a source of fear among most other Americans. Doster was a leading candidate among the Populists for the senatorial elections of both 1891 and 1893 and was elected chief justice of the Kansas Supreme Court in 1896, following his promise that, "if elected, though hampered by technical decisions in the interests of wealth, I will diligently search the books to find some law through which the interests of the common people

political life in the party of Lincoln, and when the Populist movement was brewing Judge Doster was in sympathy with it. He talked on appropriate occasions for it and his mental equipment made him a power for good.

Judge Doster was peculiarly well qualified for Senatorial duties. His legal training would have placed him early among the great lawyers of the Senate; his judicial turn would have commanded the respect of his associates in that body; and his sterling honor would have won confidence, while his clean life and modest demeanor would have reflected credit upon the people that sent him there.

Judge Doster ought to have been chosen Senator in place of Martin for two other reasons. First, because he was the best equipped Populist in the State for the place occupied by Senator Plumb, and, second, because the Senator then in office from Kansas was a Populist and a warm personal friend of Doster, and his influence in the Senate would have been greatly strengthened by the presence and congenial assistance of his campaign associate among the people.

This last mentioned consideration is of vastly more importance than it may appear to careless observers. Messrs. Ingalls and Plumb made names for themselves and glory for Kansas. They belonged to the same political party and were personally fond of each other, though unlike in almost everything. They not only worked in harmony, but

may be subserved." The conservative Republican editor of the *Atchison Globe* attacked Doster as "an anarchist and socialist of the first classs, and about as fit to be chief justice of Kansas as a hog is to teach polite manners." William Allen White condemned Doster as a "shabby, wild-eyed, rattle-brained fanatic." As his biographer has noted, however, Doster's "rhetorical radicalism" was balanced by a "legal conservatism," and neither the hopes of his supporters nor the fears of his enemies were fully realized during Doster's six-year tenure on the supreme court. Despite growing respect for his performance, he was not reelected in 1902. Thereafter, he joined the Democratic party and remained an iconoclastic voice for reform through the 1920s. For a perceptive biography, see Michael J. Brodhead, *Persevering Populist: The Life of Frank Doster* (Reno: University of Nevada Press, 1969). For the above quotations, see pages 94, 96, 102.

their joint efforts were always employed in anything that would strengthen their party or add to the credit and renown of the State.

The going of Judge Martin, Democrat, to the Senate made political agreement between the two Kansas Senators impossible, and only served to bring additional ridicule on the State, which was quite unnecessary. Upon Senator Martin's appearance in Washington the senior Senator expressed to him a hope that the two might work together in accord, especially in the matter of appointments, this on the presumption that, having been elected by Populists, he would feel under obligations to them.

But Senator Martin did not understand the matter in that way. He was elected as a Democrat, and he expected to act as a Democrat. His rooms at the National Hotel were crowded day and night with men of his own party seeking his assistance in procuring places for them in the public service. He had two experienced clerks assisting him, and they fell far behind in their work because there was so much of it. Several times the Senator had to seek rest by remaining out of the city over Sunday.

That was not the worst of it. Applications of favorite Democrats began to reach the senior Senator, and in order to overcome or neutralize his pronounced Populist proclivities these applications were accompanied by letters of recommendation from prominent members of the Populist party, even as high up as the Governor and other State officers. Within five feet of where these words are written lies a package of original letters of the character just described. These distinguished Populists did not recommend men of their own party, but in every instance the applicants were Democrats. And all this, too, before the Democratic party had got farther along with its reforms than to the election of Grover Cleveland.

Here are copies of a few of the letters referred to:

Populist State officers recommending appointment of Mr. Cooke[15] for recognition by the administration in consideration of

15. Peffer was especially outraged by any Populist solicitude for Sidney

his having withdrawn as a Democrat candidate for Congress, leaving the field clear for the Populist:

Topeka, Kansas, February 23, 1893.—To the Hon. W. A. Peffer and the Hon. John Martin and the members of the House of Representatives from Kansas—Gentlemen: Permit me to acknowledge the valuable services rendered by the Hon. Sidney G. Cooke for the success of the fusion ticket in Kansas. Mr. Cooke having been the nominee of the Democratic party of the Fifth Congressional District of Kansas, withdrew from the same and did noble work for the Hon. John Davis and thereby secured his election. Believing that Mr. Cooke is ever ready to enter a gallant fight with the opposition to defeat the Republican party of Kansas, and having done so in the last campaign, we deem it proper that he be recognized by the administration. Mr. Cooke is a good lawyer, an honorable, upright gentleman, popular with the people of Kansas and with the present administration of Kansas. Hoping that Mr. Cooke may receive a favorable consideration, we are respectfully yours,

L. D. LEWELLING, Governor,[16]

Cooke. Not only was he a conservative banker with no sympathy for Populist economic proposals, Cooke was also a leading opponent of one of Peffer's most cherished political objectives, woman suffrage, which Cooke denounced as "wrong in principle whether the women wish to vote or not and another attempt to subvert natural laws for political principles" (quoted in *Topeka Daily Capital*, June 16, 1894). Cooke himself, moreover, had opposed fusion with the Populists earlier in 1892, before bowing to political expediency, and would take a hostile stance again in 1894, after these Populist endorsements in 1893. Indeed, he ran against the Populists in 1894 as the Democratic nominee for lieutenant governor.

16. Lorenzo D. Lewelling, the Populist governor from 1893 to 1895, was a Wichita merchant who had become the chair of the Sedgwick County People's party in 1890. A sensitive and articulate champion of the

R. S. OSBORN, Secretary of State,[17]
VAN B. PRATHER, Auditor of State,[18]
JOHN T. LITTLE, Attorney General,[19]
W. H. BIDDLE, State Treasurer,[20]

oppressed, he nevertheless built his political career upon political compromises that produced little achievement but significant opposition. His conservative and inactive role as a state senator in 1897, for instance, brought him criticism as a "Judas of Populism."

17. Russell Scott Osborn of Stockton, Kansas, had been a Congregational minister in Osborne County for many years before moving to Rooks County as a farmer in 1890. A former Republican, he then joined the People's party and was nominated for secretary of state on the first Populist ticket in 1890. He was a delegate to the Cincinnati conference that launched the national People's party in 1891 and was chosen to represent Kansas on the Populist National Committee. Nominated again for secretary of state in 1892, he was this time elected. After falling out with Governor Lewelling, he was not renominated by the Populists in 1894.

18. Van B. Prather was a Cherokee County farmer and stockraiser who was the state lecturer of the Farmers' Alliance and, for a time, the editor of the *Alliance Tribune*. He had been a Democrat before affiliating with the People's party (and still ran as the Democratic nominee for a local office in 1891). Nominated by both Populists and Democrats, he was elected state auditor in 1892, but he was defeated for reelection in 1894. In 1896 Prather moved to Kansas City, Kansas, where he eventually became a prominent Democrat and the probate judge of Wyandotte County.

19. John T. Little of Olathe had been a Democrat until 1876 when he joined the first of a succession of third parties. He was elected on the Greenback ticket to two terms as the prosecuting attorney of Johnson County in the 1880s and also served as the city attorney of Olathe. As a Populist in 1892 Little actively promoted fusion with the Democrats and was elected attorney general after receiving nominations from both parties. In 1894 he was nominated to the state supreme court but failed of election. Thereafter he returned to the Democratic party.

20. William H. Biddle of Augusta was a Butler County farmer who was elected state president of the Farmers' Alliance in 1891. He had been a Republican until 1886 when he joined the Prohibitionists, and in 1890 he helped organize the People's party. He was three times nominated by the Populists for state treasurer, in 1890, 1892, and 1894, and was elected in 1892 when the Democrats nominated him as well.

H. N. GAINES, Supt. of Pub. Instruction.[21]

Letters of leading Populists recommending Frank S. Thomas[22] for postmaster at Topeka in consideration of campaign services. Letter of the Hon. W. A. Harris, Congressman-elect at Large:

Linwood, Kansas, February 4, 1893—The Hon. W. A. Peffer, Washington, D.C.—My Dear Sir: I desire heartily to recommend the appointment of Mr. Frank S. Thomas as Postmaster at Topeka. Mr. Thomas from the first publicly and conspicuously advocated fusion of the forces arrayed against the Republican party and he has at all times worked zealously to bring about the result which has been so gratifying. He is doubtless fully and favorably known by you, and I will only add that I feel sure that his appointment will be of great value in the future and will give general satisfaction. Truly yours,

W. A. HARRIS

21. Henry N. Gaines of Salina, a former Democrat, was a graduate of the Kansas State Normal School and, at the time of his election as Kansas Superintendent of Public Instruction in 1892, a professor at Central Normal College at Salina.

22. Like Cooke, Frank S. Thomas seemed to Peffer to represent a particularly flagrant example of the moral morass of fusion. Thomas was the leader of the local Democrats in Shawnee County and, following these endorsements by Populist as well as Democratic officeholders, he was appointed postmaster of Topeka. He promptly violated civil service law by firing all Republican postal carriers and otherwise behaved so outrageously that the Cleveland administration was compelled to remove him from office. In 1894, Shawnee County Democrats, still under his control, denounced "New England mugwumps" for causing the removal of Thomas and resolved against the civil service law. Thomas himself then rejected fusion in that year's campaign while promising to support it again in 1896 if it would promote the interests of the Democratic party. See *Topeka Daily Capital*, July 1, 6, 1894.

Letter of John W. Breidenthal,[23] chairman of the Populist State Central Committee and State Bank Commissioner:

Topeka, Kansas, March 9, 1893. The Hon. W. A. Peffer, Washington, D.C.—My Dear Senator: Being now a patron of the Topeka post office and a resident of the city, I take the liberty of addressing you regarding the appointment of a postmaster. During the late campaign I became acquainted with quite a number of the prominent Democrats of the city, and among them Mr. Frank S. Thomas, who is now an applicant for the above named appointment, and I take pleasure in saying that in my opinion there is no one more deserving of recognition at the hands of the present administration than is Mr. Thomas. He was an earnest, active, and energetic supporter of our entire State ticket, never losing an opportunity to advocate and defend our cause as against the Republicans. That his appointment would be a good one from a political standpoint I have not the slightest doubt, and that he would make an efficient and accommodating official I am equally confident. Should you be able to assist Mr. Thomas in secur-

23. John Breidenthal of Chetopa and Topeka was a banker and real estate developer who nevertheless affiliated with a series of radical third parties. He was the Greenback nominee for lieutenant governor in 1884 and chaired the Union Labor party in 1887 and 1888. An "organizational genius of sorts," in the words of Gene Clanton, Breidenthal then joined the Populists and in 1892 replaced Levi Dumbauld as chair of the state party, a position he retained for most of the 1890s and used consistently to promote fusion. He was so successful in achieving that objective that frustrated antifusion Populists denounced Breidenthal as "the most collossal [*sic*] aggregation of political cussedness on earth." He served two four-year terms as state banking commissioner and in 1900 was the fusion nominee of both Populists and Democrats for governor. See O. Gene Clanton, *Kansas Populism: Ideas and Men* (Lawrence: University Press of Kansas, 1969), 121 (first quotation); and Walter T. K. Nugent, *The Tolerant Populists: Kansas Populism and Nativism* (Chicago: University of Chicago Press, 1963), 138 (second quotation).

ing this appointment you would confer a favor on his friends and materially aid our party in the future. Very truly yours, JOHN W. BREIDENTHAL.

Letter of Governor L. D. Lewelling:

Topeka, Kansas, March 7, 1893.—[Dictated]—The Hon. W. A. Peffer, Washington, D.C.—My Dear Sir: Frank S. Thomas of this city is seeking the appointment of postmaster. It seems presumptuous on my part to write letters in behalf of persons who live in your own city and where you are so much better acquainted, but so far as I hear and know the appointment of Mr. Thomas would give satisfaction to the people of Topeka. My acquaintance with Mr. Thomas is limited, but I am well satisfied that he is an excellent citizen and a good, strong, and worthy Democrat; and it is only fair to presume that any favors on your part to secure his appointment would be appreciated by the people here. Yours respectfully,   L. D. LEWELLING, Governor.

This line of policy at once made it impossible for the Populist Senator to do anything in the way of appointments for his political friends. The few for whom he had secured places were relieved and Democrats got their places.

The two Kansas Senators could not work together politically. Personally they were on the most friendly terms, but politically they were enemies. The Populist Senator did not recommend any of the Democratic applicants whether they had armed themselves with letters from Populist head men or not. He had supposed that Populism meant reform, and when Populists had sent a Senator up to look after the personal interests of members of the Democratic party that Senator was just the man for such work.

V
Populists and Democrats in Congress

In the preamble to the national platform of the Populist party, adopted at Omaha on July 4, 1892, are these words:

> We have witnessed for more than a quarter of a century the struggles of the two great political parties for power and plunder, while grievous wrongs have been inflicted on the suffering people. We charge that the controlling influences dominating both these parties have permitted the existing dreadful conditions to develop without serious effort to prevent or restrain them. Neither do they now promise us any substantial reform. They have agreed together to ignore in the coming campaign every issue but one. They propose to drown the outcries of a plundered people with the uproar of a sham battle over the tariff, so that capitalists, corporations, national banks, rings, trusts, watered stock, the demonetization of silver, and the oppressions of the usurers may all be lost sight of. They propose to sacrifice our homes, lives, and children on the altar of mammon; to destroy the multitude in order to secure corruption funds from the millionaires.

That is a serious arraignment, and it could not have been adopted by the convention had it not included both the Republican and Democratic parties, because the membership of the body was composed of men that had belonged in both of them. The farmers' organizations, out of which the new party had grown, were nonpartisan bodies, made up of men and women of all shades of political belief.

The Populist party set out on a line between the two great parties, opposed to both of them, and was treated accordingly as the enemy of both. In the formation of committees of the Senate and House, Populists were put either in the middle, between the Republican and Democratic members, or at the end of the minority members. And they were not put on any of the leading committees, nor on any whose duties lay in the domain of party politics.

[Populists in Congress in 1891]

The Fifty-second Congress, the term of which began on March 4, 1891, was the first to have any Populists in its membership. In the Senate Peffer of Kansas was the only member chosen by the People's party and calling himself a Populist. He was assigned to five different standing committees and was placed exactly in the middle of four of them and between four Republicans and three Democrats on the fifth. Kyle of South Dakota styled himself an Independent. He was placed on three standing committees and three select committees and was put among the Democratic members of such of them as had more than three Senators, and in the middle of such as had only three. Irby of South Carolina, although President of the State Alliance and elected through the influence and votes of the order, classed himself a Democrat. He was elected as such; for at the time of his election the Populist movement had not begun in the South.

Republicans were then in majority and had control in committees, as well as in the Senate, and nothing occurred during either of the two sessions of that Congress to change or affect the attitude of either the Republican or the Democratic parties toward the few

In 1891 Peffer entered the Senate as its first Populist member, and his caricature made its national debut in this cartoon by Frederick Burr Opper (Puck, April 8, 1891). Peffer was not insensitive to such portrayals. In an early speech in the Senate, he noted that an older senator had suggested "that those of us who venture to discuss this question before we have become warm in this Chamber should tarry at Jericho, as certain of our ancestors had been advised to do, until their beards had grown. If the newspaper and magazine caricatures are to be taken in evidence, I have been at Jericho some time." (Congressional Record, 53d Cong., 1st sess., Appendix p. 34)

Populists in Congress. There were only six[1] of them in the House to 350 members of the great parties, and one in the Senate to eighty-six Republicans and Democrats.

There was little then, except in Congress, to cause alarm among

1. This number is incorrect. As Peffer indicates above on page 51, there were nine Populists in the first House.

politicians on account of possible defections from either party. Democrats had control of the Alliance in all the Southern States until the early summer of 1892, and no political action had that year could alter the party complexion of the Fifty-second Congress, which did not expire until March 3, 1893. The Populist contingent in both Houses was so small and inconsequential, and its party doctrines so new and radical, that it could be, as it was, safely regarded as fit only for ridicule by both parties.

When it became evident that the success of the Democratic ticket, with ex-President Cleveland at its head, would reduce Democratic majorities in the Southern States, and that Democratic loss there was Populist gain, the leading members of the successful party in 1892 were bitter in denunciation of all Democrats that had been or were likely to be affected with the contagion of Populism. In the long debates on the bill to repeal the purchasing clause of the Sherman silver law and on the Wilson tariff bill, men like Hill,[2] Vest,[3] and Mills[4] used Populism as a cat-o'-nine-tails over the backs of shaky and hesitating Democrats. Hill directly charged the Kan-

2. David B. Hill was a Democratic senator and former governor from New York. He was a vitriolic opponent of Populism and constantly sparred with Peffer on the Senate floor. For a time he expediently dabbled with bimetallism as a tactic to contest the Democratic presidential nomination with Cleveland in 1892, but he always remained a conservative rigorously committed to Democratic principles of negative government, and he was the leading speaker in behalf of the gold plank at the 1896 Democratic National Convention. His rather loose political morality frequently shocked Peffer in the Senate and convinced another observer that Hill was "the worst man a political party in America has ever offered for popular suffrage." Quoted in H. Wayne Morgan, *From Hayes to McKinley: National Party Politics, 1877–1896* (Syracuse, N.Y.: Syracuse University Press, 1969), 408.

3. George G. Vest of Missouri had been a member of the Confederate Congress and served as a Democratic senator in Washington from 1879 to 1903. In 1890 he had signed a card like that Peffer describes for North Carolina on page 53, pledging to support the demands of the Farmers' Alliance, but his modest reform interests were limited to the tariff and international bimetallism, and he resolutely rejected third-party action.

AWAITING THE NEWS FROM WASHINGTON.

Endorsing the gold standard, this cartoon sympathetically portrays a New York financier, disconsolate in the 1893 panic, while Peffer and Missouri Democrat George Vest lead the Senate filibuster against the repeal of the Sherman Silver Purchase Act. Despite Vest's support for silver, Peffer describes him as otherwise a bitter opponent of Populism and concludes that such Silver Democrats had no use for Populists (in or out of Congress) "except their votes." (Puck, August 30, 1893) sas Senator with a deliberate purpose to break up the Democratic party (and the charge was not denied), and he used that argument as a lash to keep his party brethren in line. Nothing within the rules of parliamentary decorum was deemed too contemptuous or severe in expressing his hatred of Populism and contempt for Democrats who allowed themselves to be contaminated with its virus.

Senator Mills of Texas in the silver debate, being chided for his support of the administration measure and charged with being in alliance with John Sherman[5] and the "goldbugs," replied:

> I do not intend to be deterred by taunts that I am serving with the Senator from Ohio [Mr. Sherman], that he is my chief. Politics makes strange bedfellows, Mr. President, and the present condition of the country throws me and a number of my brethren on this side in company with the distinguished Senator from Ohio. But where does it throw the other gentlemen? Under the leadership of the distinguished Senator from Kansas [Mr. Peffer]. Mr. President, it is a question of taste, very much, about these things. There is an unwritten law—

For his pledge, see Homer Clevenger, "The Farmers' Alliance in Missouri," *Missouri Historical Review* 39 (October 1944): 40.

4. Roger Q. Mills of Texas served in the House of Representatives from 1873 to 1892 and in the Senate from 1892 to 1899. A staunch Democrat, he was known as a "Confederate Brigadier" for his old fashioned politics emphasizing limited government and a low tariff, the latter of which was embodied in the famous Mills Bill of 1888. He was a firm opponent of free silver and committed ally of Grover Cleveland.

5. John Sherman of Mansfield, Ohio, secretary of the Treasury under President Hayes from 1877 to 1881 and United States Senator from 1861 to 1877 and 1881 to 1897, was the leading Republican advocate of "sound money" and the major architect of the postwar financial policies condemned by Greenbackers and Populists. Ironically, in light of subsequent developments, in 1870 Peffer, then a loyal Republican, and his wife, Sarah Jane, named a son after Sherman. Although this ignominious burden was perhaps not responsible, John Sherman Peffer had an unhappy life, fell victim to the bottle, and committed suicide in 1899.

no, it is written—*de gustibus non est disputandum.* Let everyone go wherever it suits him. The Senator from Ohio and those who are acting with him on his side of the Chamber are standing for the old Democratic doctrine of sound currency, gold, silver, and paper at par all over the country. I give him my hand in this contest. The Senator from Kansas is contending for overturning the whole system of finance, issuing paper money, and lifting the business of the country in the air on paper money, bidding adieu to the basis of gold and silver. He is for Government ownership of railroads and telegraphs, and perhaps every other thing that it can find lying loose around about in the country. If there is more affinity, if there is more attachment and kinship for the doctrine of the Senator from Kansas, I say to my friends, go as you like. I shall stand with those who stand for a sound and stable currency and nothing short of that.—(See *Congressional Record*, vol. 25, part 3, page 2,655).

[Populists under Cleveland]

With the beginning of the Cleveland administration Democrats had a majority in both Houses, and they were more liberal with the Populists, especially in the Senate. Allen[6] of Nebraska came in then. He is not classed as a member of any party in the *Congressional Directory*, but he claimed to be a Populist. Then there were three Senators who were not in accord with either of the great parties, and each of them was made chairman of one commit-

6. William V. Allen, a lawyer and judge from Madison County, Nebraska, was elected to the Senate in 1893 by the Populist-Democratic coalition that controlled the Nebraska legislature. As Peffer notes below, Allen was rather conservative for a Populist. He was described by one Republican newspaper, for example, as not a "hair-brained visionary or wild-eyed revolutionist. Quite the contrary . . . he is . . . well-balanced, broad-

tee, which added somewhat to the Senator's dignity and gave his clerk additional salary.

These three Senators had occasional conferences, and were in the main agreed upon a line of policy. They occasionally met with the Populist members of the House in consultation, and together they had formed what seemed to be a nucleus around which Populists could gather in the future as a separate and distinct party in Congress. Being the first and, up to that time, the only party that made an issue of the silver question by demanding free and unlimited coinage at the present ratio, Populists were prepared at the outset to oppose the policy of President Cleveland when he called Congress together on August 7, 1893, to repeal so much of the Sherman law as directed the purchase and coinage of silver bullion, and their attitude in that matter brought them into accord with such of the Democrats as did not agree with the President in his opposition to silver. The longer the debate continued the more alike became the speeches of Populists and silver Democrats. Senator Mills had the correct diagnosis of the situation, as he expressed it in the language above quoted from one of his speeches. This harmony and cooperation in the silver fight opened the way for friendly interchanges of opinions when the Wilson tariff bill came on to be considered, and it was not until then that any appreciable effort was made on the part of Democrats in Congress to secure Populist support of any party measure. The Democratic majority was not large in either House, and votes were in demand.

The three Populist Senators agreed upon the outlines of a bill which they would support, and the Senator from Kansas was requested to prepare it. His bill became Senate bill No. 1,762, and

minded, and *conservative*" (quoted in Karel D. Bicha, *Western Populism: Studies in an Ambivalent Conservatism* [Lawrence, Kans.: Coronado Press, 1976], 43). Although Allen was a former Republican, he worked closely with Democrats, particularly William Jennings Bryan, and always promoted fusion. His personal opposition to the subtreasury, fiat paper money, and other Populist demands made it easy for him to accept the compromises that fusion with the Democrats entailed.

was introduced on March 12, 1894. It was entitled: "A bill to amend the customs laws and to provide additional revenue for the support of the government, and for other purposes." It proposed to reduce duties on all articles in general use among people that earn their living by hard labor, and all sorts of coarse goods used in everyday wear were put on the free list, with sugar, salt, lumber, and coal. A duty of eight cents a pound was left on combing and clothing wool. Provision was made for a graduated [income] tax, such as was demanded in the Populist party platform. (The House bill provided for taxing all incomes over $4,000 at the same rate per cent.)

As first drawn and introduced the Wilson (tariff) bill did not propose to tax incomes. A separate bill had been prepared making provision for an income tax. When Populists of the House were asked to support the tariff bill they demanded that the income tax bill be included, making one bill cover both the customs and income features. Their demand was complied with, and, that secured, they voted for the bill solidly.

When the bill came to the Senate from the House it provided for free sugar and free wool, leaving high duties on goods manufactured from wool; and the bill as a whole, subject to a few suggested amendments, was satisfactory to Messrs. Allen and Kyle, but not to the Senator from Kansas, who demanded changes to include the provisions of the bill he had prepared as the Populist bill.

The bill went at once to the Finance Committee, and when it was reported to the Senate the sugar schedule was so amended as to provide for levying a duty of one cent and upward on the pound, according to grade. The bill was afterward amended in the Senate, on motion of Senator Jones[7] of Arkansas, who had charge of the bill, so as to provide for an ad valorem duty of 40 per cent; and one-eighth of a cent a pound on certain grades was added later, in

7. James K. Jones was a lawyer and planter from Hempstead County,

*A sketch of Peffer in the Senate during the 1894 debates over tariff and income tax legislation. (*Harper's Weekly, *March 10, 1894)*

which form it passed the Senate by the votes of the Democratic members, excepting Hill of New York, whose opposition was based on objections to the income tax provision. Allen and Kyle of the

Arkansas. A Confederate veteran, he had served in the state legislature in the 1870s and in the House of Representatives in the early 1880s before be-

Populists voted aye and Peffer no on the passage of the bill. The sugar tax as finally adopted was the demand of the sugar trust—so charged and not denied.[8]

From that time forward the Populists in the House always voted with the Democrats on party questions; but in the Senate the members of that party voted independently, as they chose.

[Silver in the Fifty-third Congress]

During the term of the Fifty-third Congress, beginning on March 4, 1893, and ending on March 3, 1895, the Democrats being in control of both Houses, they reorganized the committees so as to

ing elected to the Senate, where he served from 1885 until 1903. He was a leading Silver Democrat and helped organize the Democratic Bimetallic Committee in 1895. In 1896 William Jennings Bryan appointed him as the chair of the Democratic National Committee. Apart from his silver commitment he had little in common with Populists, whom he fought vigorously in Arkansas. Populists, in turn, denounced him as "a strong representative of the worst type of Bourbon Democracy" (quoted in Stanley L. Jones, *The Presidential Election of 1896* [Madison: University of Wisconsin Press, 1964], 298).

8. When the tariff bill was under consideration in the Senate, several newspapers reported that the American Sugar Refining Company—the "sugar trust"—was lobbying actively to shape the sugar provisions and unduly influencing important senators, first through campaign contributions and then with preferential stock deals. Peffer proposed an official investigation of the charges, but the Senate rejected his proposal. As public clamor mounted, however, the Senate finally did authorize such an investigation, which revealed that several senators had in fact speculated in sugar stocks while the bill was pending. Public outrage was not lessened when one such senator announced, "I do not feel that there is anything in my connection with the Senate to interfere with my buying or selling the stock when I please, and I propose to do so in the future." Under the careful questioning of Populist Senator Allen, the Senate investigation also produced startling evidence of corporate campaign contributions to both Democrats and Republicans. See Harold U. Faulkner, *Politics, Reform, and Expansion, 1890–1900* (New York: Harper & Row, 1959), 158–161.

have a Democratic majority on all the important ones. Senator Voorhees[9] of Indiana, a Democrat of great distinction and a leader in his party many years, was chairman of the Senate Committee on Finance, and in that capacity he had charge of the repeal bill during the long debate at the extra session in '93. Being known as a friend of silver, he was confronted while the debate was on with his record on that subject, and he answered that he was opposed to buying silver to coin; that he favored the bill proposing to stop the purchasing business because he wanted free and unlimited coinage; and he said that he would favor a free coinage bill if brought before the Senate as a subject by itself.

Whether it was to make that pledge good as a party obligation need not now be asked or discussed, but a few weeks before the adjournment of the Fifty-third Congress—to-wit: on June 23, 1895—Senator Jones of Arkansas introduced Senate Bill No. 2642, entitled: "A bill providing for the issue of bonds, the coinage of silver, and for other purposes." The bill was doubtless intended to bring the Democratic party together on the silver question, for several bills of a somewhat similar character had been introduced in the House.

This Jones bill was advertised in the newspapers of the country as a silver bill, and, coming at that time and from that source, the people expected a renewal of the struggle for free silver. But it was nothing of that kind, as an inspection of the bill will disclose. Here is a copy of all that is material in the first section of the bill:

> Be it enacted, etc., That authority is hereby given to the Secretary of the Treasury to issue bonds of the United States to the amount of $500,000,000, coupon or registered, at the option of the buyer, payable, principal and interest, in coin of

9. Daniel W. Voorhees was a veteran Democrat revered by his Indiana constituents as "the Tall Sycamore of the Wabash." After serving in the House in the 1860s, he represented his state in the Senate from 1877 to 1897. His peculiar course in the struggle over repeal was determined by Grover Cleveland's determined use of federal patronage.

the present standard value, and bearing interest at the rate of 3 per cent per annum, payable quarterly, and not to be sold at less than par, the bonds to mature thirty years from date, and be redeemable at the option of the government after twenty years; and that the Secretary of the Treasury be, and he is hereby, authorized to use the proceeds of the sale of said bonds to defray current expenses of the government, and for the redemption of United States legal tender Treasury notes, issued under the act of July 14, 1890, as hereinafter provided . . . . Whenever the Secretary of the Treasury shall offer any of the bonds herein authorized for sale he shall advertise the same and authorize subscriptions therefor to be made at the Treasury department . . . it being the intention of this act to give full and free opportunity for the general subscription, and payment therefor may be made in gold coin, but the Secretary of the Treasury may, in his discretion, accept in payment therefor United States legal tender notes and Treasury notes issued under the act of July 14, 1890.

Section 2 provides that national banks may issue circulating notes to the par value of the bonds deposited as security, and the tax on circulation is reduced to one-fourth of 1 per cent per annum. Sections 3, 4, 5, and 6 relate to details of national banking. Section 7 provides: "That the Secretary of the Treasury is hereby authorized and directed, out of the proceeds of the sale of the bonds as hereinbefore provided, to cancel and destroy all United States legal tender notes and Treasury notes issued under the act of July 14, 1890, of less denominations than $10, and to issue a like amount of silver certificates, etc." Section 8 provides further details of redemption of notes.

There were ten sections in the bill. The tenth and last section authorized the Secretary to prescribe suitable rules and regulations to carry out the provisions of the bill.

Section 9 is the silver section, and is as follows:

Section 9. That from and after the passage of this act the Secretary of the Treasury is hereby authorized and directed to receive at any United States mint, from any citizen of the United States, silver bullion of standard fineness and coin the same into dollars of 412 1/2 grains each. The seigniorage on the said bullion shall belong to the United States, and shall be the difference between the coinage value thereof and the price of the bullion at London on the day the deposit is made, and all expenditures for coinage done under the provisions of this act shall be paid out of said seigniorage; and the Secretary of the Treasury shall deliver to the depositors of such bullion standard silver dollars equal in amount to the price thereof as aforesaid; and whenever the said coins herein provided for shall be received into the Treasury certificates in denominations of less than $10 may be issued thereon, in the manner now provided by law.

The bill was referred to the Finance Committee, of which Senator Jones, the author of the bill, was a member, assisted by the following named Senators, all Democrats: Voorhees of Indiana, McPherson of New Jersey,[10] Harris of Tennessee,[11] Vest of Missouri, and White of California.[12] Adding Mr. Jones of Arkansas, we have the names of six men of influence in the Democratic party who, when they came to act on [the] bill, struck out all but the silver section and reported that to the Senate, with the word "market" in-

10. John R. McPherson was a Democratic senator from New Jersey from 1877 to 1895. He was one of those senators implicated in the investigation of the sugar lobby with having purchased sugar stock while the Wilson tariff was pending.

11. Isham G. Harris was an old-line Democrat who first went to Congress in 1849. In 1861 he had been the secessionist governor of Tennessee. After the Civil War, he was a leading Redeemer and Bourbon Democrat. He served in the Senate from 1877 until his death in 1897. He was a vitriolic opponent of the Farmers' Alliance demands, which he denounced as "subversive of every principle" of the Democratic party, and constantly at-

serted before "price"; the word "London" stricken out and "New York" inserted; the words "in denominations of less than ten dollars" stricken out, and the title of the bill amended so as to read, "A bill providing for the unrestricted coinage of silver and for other purposes."

The bill was drawn with the expectation that it would unite the Democrats; and, with the bond provisions stricken out, it was expected that it would receive the entire silver vote of the Senate. The Finance Committee consisted of eleven members—the six Democrats above named and five Republicans—Morrill of Vermont,[13] Sherman of Ohio, Jones of Nevada,[14] Allison of Iowa,[15] and Aldrich of Rhode Island.[16] The Republican members of the committee

tacked the People's party (quoted in Roger L. Hart, *Redeemers, Bourbons, and Populists: Tennessee, 1870–1896* [Baton Rouge: Louisiana State University Press, 1975], 148).

12. After serving prominently in the California state legislature from 1880 to 1890, Stephen Mallory White was elected to the United States Senate in 1893. White was a leading Silver Democrat and was chosen the permanent chair of the 1896 Democratic National Convention.

13. Justin S. Morrill served in Congress from 1855 until 1898. The author of the Morrill Land Grant Act of 1862, he was a fierce protectionist and an opponent of monetary reform.

14. After making a fortune in mining, John P. Jones represented Nevada in the Senate from 1873 until 1903. For both personal and political reasons he was absolutely committed to free silver, and in 1894 he renounced his ties to the Republican party and declared himself a Populist. He candidly admitted, however, that he shared no other principles with the Populists, and he worked closely with the American Bimetallic League and with silver politicians of all parties to bring about a fusion campaign in 1896.

15. William B. Allison was one of the leading Republicans in the Senate, where he represented Iowa from 1873 to 1908. A financial conservative, he had helped block free silver with the Bland-Allison Act of 1878 and thereafter continued to use his influence and parliamentary skills to frustrate the advocates of monetary reform.

16. Nelson W. Aldrich of Rhode Island was a prominent member of the Senate's inner circle. A reactionary Republican who ruthlessly dominated Rhode Island politics and promoted business interests, Aldrich pre-

unanimously opposed the bill, and the Democratic members were all in its favor, giving one vote majority for reporting the bill favorably. McPherson of New Jersey, representing the gold wing of the party, said he was satisfied with the bill.

Mr. Jones reported the bill to the Senate on February 12, and asked for its immediate consideration, but on objection the bill went to the calendar. On February 18 Mr. Jones moved to take up the bill, and after some sparring the motion prevailed, when Mr. Jones asked for an immediate vote, being satisfied that he had a majority of the Senate with him. He did not get a vote, however, but at every opportunity he and other Democratic friends of the measure urged a vote, until it became evident that a vote could not be had during the session, for there were only a few days left, and several of the large appropriation bills had yet to be considered and disposed of.

On the 20th Mr. Jones ceased his efforts, saying: "Developments have shown that while the friends of the measure have a majority in this body it is impossible to pass the bill at the present late day in the session without incurring grave danger to the appropriation bills and an extra session. Under the circumstances the friends of the silver measure have authorized me to say that it will not be further pressed at this session of Congress."

As further evidence that this bill was prepared as a party measure, Mr. Jones, when he introduced it, submitted a few observations, from which the following is quoted:

> I am in favor of the broadest silver legislation. I would be in favor of a much more radical silver measure than I have proposed in this bill, but we all know the utter impossibility of the extreme silver men putting into law their views at this time. I believe the silver men will make a mistake now—a great mistake—if by insisting on a more extreme and radical measure than the one I have proposed they render it impossible to ac-

ferred to work quietly behind the scenes in favor of protectionism and sound money.

complish anything at all. I believe the enactment of this bill into law will be a great stride forward in the interest of silver; that, once recognized, silver will assert and maintain itself, and that it will bring great relief to the masses of the people. I believe it ought to commend itself to the good judgment of Senators who are considering the welfare of the people as well as the condition of the Treasury of the United States, and to my mind the condition of the people is of infinitely more importance than the other. (See *Congressional Record*, vol. 27, part 2, page 1,249.)

On the page last preceding (1248), same volume and part, relative to the retirement and cancellation of greenbacks, as provided in this bill, Mr. Jones is on record as saying: "Now, Mr. President, the proposition to retire the greenbacks is one that a good many persons seem to have some hesitancy about. The reason given is that the greenbacks are a money of the people; that it is a popular currency. Twenty years ago that was a fact; it was true ten years ago, but it is not so now."

There were four features in that bill which were in direct opposition to Populist doctrine—retirement of greenback currency, permanency of the national bank system, measuring the value of silver by gold, and coining dollars according to the market value of bullion. There was at least one Populist vote in the Senate that would not have been recorded in favor of the bill.

Democrats in Congress were always ready to avail themselves of Populist support, but they seemed to be as much opposed to political affiliation with the new party as white men in the South are averse to the intermeddling of negroes in public affairs. All overtures from Populists looking toward formation of a new party under a new name and creed, to be composed of voters who were agreed on the silver question, were repelled.

When the first session of the Fifty-fourth Congress was about to meet in December, 1895, the Populist Senators proposed to organize the Senate on silver lines, and they sent to each of the Senators of the other parties known to be favorable to silver legislation the following notice and invitation:

> Washington, D.C., November 30, 1895. Hon—Dear Sir: There will be a meeting of Senators friendly to silver in the Marble Room of the Capitol on Monday, December 2 at 11 a.m., to consult with a view of organizing the Senate on silver lines. You are respectfully invited to attend.
> W. M. STEWART.[17]
> W. V. ALLEN.
> W. A. PEFFER.
> MARION BUTLER.[18]

There were then fifty-two Senators who were more or less friendly to silver, each and all of whom were thus officially invited to attend the conference, and seats were prepared for that number;

17. William M. Stewart, like John P. Jones, had been a Republican senator from Nevada whose obsession with silver coinage caused him to join the People's party in the mid 1890s and thereafter consistently work to undermine the party in order to bring about political fusion on the solitary basis of silver.

18. Marion Butler was the youngest member of the Senate, having been born in 1863, but he was already a skilled politician. Butler had been elected as an Alliance Democrat to the North Carolina legislature in 1890 and thereafter joined the Populists, serving in turn as both the state and the national chair of the People's party. He fashioned a fusion with North Carolina Republicans in 1894 that placed him in the Senate, where he was an eloquent champion of Populist economic and political reform principles.

The two other Populist senators in 1895, James H. Kyle of South Dakota and John P. Jones of Nevada, did not sign the invitation printed above because they had not yet arrived in Washington for the new session of Congress. According to Butler, they both later endorsed the message. For Butler's account of this development, see *Congressional Record*, 54th Cong., 1st sess., December 30, 1895, p. 425.

but at the time appointed and during the hour which could have been occupied in consultation (11 to 12) two Democratic and three Republican Senators called to pay their respects and say they had no desire or intention to disturb their own party lines. The proposed conference was an utter failure.

VI
Birth and Death of the
Proposed Silver Party

During the period of the first session of the Fifty-fourth Congress, beginning in December, 1895, and more especially during the first half of the session, silver was the principal topic of discussion at the national capital. The failure to get a vote on the Jones bill at the last preceding session and the consequent loss of opportunity to unite the Democratic party on a silver policy that could be safely defended before the country, taken in connection with the fact that the silver tide was flowing and silver champions were waxing more radical with the passing time, and in consideration of the further fact that Populists then claimed to have a voting power equal to about 2,000,000 ballots—and their party was the first and up to that time the only party that had put the silver question in issue—it was necessary, if success were to be sought as among possible achievements, to devise some means whereby the friends of silver could be brought into concerted action outside the Populist party.

In his speeches in the Senate the Kansas Populist [Peffer] had several times availed himself of the opportunity to suggest and to urge a union of the silver vote of the country through the formation of a new party pledged to monetary reform, making silver the rallying cry. Here is one of many similar expressions of his on that line:

I want to say to Senators that they need not fear that any great harm will come to the country by reason of the predicted disintegration of the two old parties. There is a bright, young, vigorous party now on the map of politics that is ready to strike hands with men of all other parties to make the fight for silver. I care not whether you call it Populist, whether you call it National, or what you call it. (*Congressional Record* of September 4, 1893, page 1,205.)

Overtures of like tenor had been made in open Senate by the same Senator before the date of this deliverance and after. And in private conversations with active silver men in other parties he urged a gathering into one new and distinct political body of all voters that were in harmony on the single question of restoring unrestricted silver coinage, leaving other questions of a reformatory character for future determination as time should develop opportunities. This proposed line of policy, of course, involved the separation of men from their present party associations. Democrats, Republicans, and Populists alike would have to leave their parties and together form another and an entirely new organization for the purpose of working out such reforms as we could, beginning on silver lines.

But party prejudices were in the way, and besides—and what was quite as controlling—there was the fact that the proposition for union came from Populists. Such a getting together could easily have been effected if men of other parties had been as liberal and zealous as those that proposed it.

But nothing could be done on that line, and Populists—the original silver men—did not see why, if party names were to be retained, the silver voters who were in the minority, and therefore helpless, in other parties, should not vote with the People's Party. And they proposed that course. The answer came in due time through Senator Dubois[1] in a speech delivered in the Senate on January 23, 1896 (to which reference will be again made later), and from other authoritative sources.

1. Fred Dubois of Idaho was elected to the Senate in 1891 as a Republi-

While the Jones bill was pending [in 1895], General Weaver, the People's Party candidate for the Presidency in 1892, went to Washington City and asked the Populist Senators and Congressmen to sign an address which he had prepared, and give it to the Associated Press for distribution. This manifesto had been written in manifold and a copy delivered to each of the parties aforesaid. After setting forth what was believed to be a clear and correct statement of the political situation at the time, the document advised Populists to "concentrate all their energies, for the time being, on the financial question."

A conference of Congressional Populists was called for the night of the day when the proposed address was presented. Only a few—among them McKeighan and Kem of Nebraska and Baker and Peffer of Kansas—met with the General. It was objected on the part of one of the gentlemen present that the advice to concentrate our forces on the financial question would occasion trouble; that the voters of the party would understand it to mean the silver question alone, which, to a Populist at that time, was only a part, and a small part at that, of the financial question. It was objected, further, that such advice just then, when looked at in the light of existing political conditions, would be regarded by Populists, and especially the more radical ones, as resulting from advances made on the part of Democrats in negotiations for Populist support. And it was still further objected that such an address from such a source, coming at the particular time, would arouse a suspicion among our voters that their representatives at Washington, whom they had sent up to procure legislation and not to run the party, were preparing to trade their constituents' votes away.

To these objections General Weaver answered that he knew the Democrats were preparing to raise the issue—the financial issue—

can. An ardent advocate of silver, he bolted the 1896 Republican National Convention upon its endorsement of the gold standard and helped form the Silver Republican party. He was elected again to the Senate in 1901 as a Silver Republican, but thereafter became a Democrat.

and he thought the wise thing for his party to do was to take the lead.

To this it was replied that the Populists were already in the lead; that they had opened the fight in 1892, and had devoted one whole plank in their national platform to silver in words too plain to be misunderstood and too few to be easily forgotten, and that if Democrats were anxious on the subject they could find a home with us and a silver platform just to their taste.

These objections were discussed by General Weaver and the objecting member of the conference for some time, when, coming to no agreement, another meeting was proposed for the next morning at the office rooms of Senator Allen. At the proposed meeting in the morning Senator Allen was not present, nor were there any persons in attendance who had anything to say on the matter in hand, excepting General Weaver and the objector of the night before; but the manifesto was present and had attached to it the signatures of all the Congressional Populists but that of the Senator from Kansas, who refused to sign, and said the party was going onto breakers, that that address was the beginning of a movement which would eventually work the ruin of Populism through the agency of the Democratic party.

Following are the names subscribed to the Weaver manifesto: Lafe Pence,[2] O. M. Kem, T. J. Hudson, William Baker, W. A. McKeighan, William V. Allen, John Davis, W. A. Harris, Jerry Simpson, J. C. Bell,[3] J. H. Kyle, H. E. Boen,[4] H. E. Taubeneck,[5] and J. B. Weaver.

2. Lafayette Pence, a Denver lawyer, was elected to the House of Representatives in 1892 as the fusion candidate of the Populists and Silver Democrats of Colorado.

3. John C. Bell was a Colorado lawyer and judge who joined the People's party. Beginning in 1892, he was elected to five terms in Congress as the Populist and Democratic fusion candidate. In 1895–1896, he was the floor leader of the House Populists.

4. Haldor E. Boen was a Norwegian immigrant who settled in Minnesota and in 1892 was elected to Congress on the Populist ticket.

The address was sent out through the press on February 14, 1895. The [National] Reform Press Association, a body of newspaper people representing Populism, held its annual session for that year ('95) at Kansas City, Missouri, on February 22, and among the topics discussed was the Congressional address above referred to, and a question was raised on the absence of the Kansas Senator's name. A committee of inquiry was appointed, with instructions to visit Washington and confer with Populists there in and out of Congress in relation to politics generally.

It so happened that the headquarters of the Populist National Committee—H. E. Taubeneck, chairman, and J. H. Turner,[6] secretary—were then in Washington.

The visiting committee were greatly pleased with their reception, and so expressed themselves in their report to the body appointing

5. Herman E. Taubeneck was the chair of the People's Party National Committee, 1891–1896. He first came to public attention as an Illinois legislator elected by the Farmers' Mutual Benefit Association in 1890 and as the only independent who refused to bolt the Senatorial candidacy of A. J. Streeter and support the Democratic candidate, John M. Palmer. That apparent show of political courage caused Populists at the 1891 Cincinnati Conference to elect him as party chair, a position for which he was completely unqualified by reason of intellect, personality, or organizational ability. A relative conservative, he opposed many distinctive Populist principles, distrusted their advocates, and tried to purge both from the party. His tactics kept the party in turmoil, prompting one Kansas Populist to censure "the double-dealing of our national chairman," and led to a series of fiascoes in 1896. The Populist National Convention in that year soundly repudiated him. (Quotation from *Girard World*, May 21, 1896.)

6. J. H. Turner, a former school teacher in Troup County, Georgia, had become secretary of the National Farmers' Alliance and Industrial Union in 1889 and then a member and secretary of the Populist National Committee. In 1895 he also became the business manager of the *Silver Knight*, a newspaper launched in Washington by Senator Stewart to promote silver politics. He then established his own journal, the *Record Review*, to accomplish the same objective. In 1896, Turner not only advocated Populist endorsement of Democratic presidential nominee William Jennings Bryan but proposed that Populists actually join the Democratic party.

them. They spent several days in the city, and the longer they remained the more confident they were that the old parties were disintegrating and the hope of the country lay in the success of the Populist movement which they thought was fast absorbing all kindred political elements. This is the way the committee handled that phase of the subject in their report:

Evidence of the most convincing character is exhibited of the general disintegration of both the old parties and a realignment of political forces. The Democratic party is demoralized and disrupted, and their allies, the Republicans, are at sea, unable to determine what this wonderful upheaval of public sentiment will bring forth. Amid all the uncertainty which beclouds the political horizon of the old parties, the Populist party, harmonious in rank and file, free from jealousies and schisms among its leaders, united in its aims and purposes, invoking the aid of the God of our fathers, unitedly confronts the enemies of the people and is marching in solid phalanx boldly and resolutely to meet the impending conflict.

The committee was entirely satisfied with the party loyalty of every man of its faith on duty in Congress, and it procured a written statement from the gentlemen who signed the manifesto of February 14 to the effect that in what they had sent out they did not mean to be understood as advising the abandonment or dropping of any doctrine of the party embodied in the platform adopted at Omaha in 1892. The report of this visiting committee was duly published by Populist papers. It can be found in the Topeka *Advocate* of March 13, 1895, at page #8.

Along in the latter part of February and early part of March (1895) silver men were in conference in Washington. Populists were not invited to attend any of the conferences, though Senator Stewart of Nevada, who was regularly in communication between Populists and Democrats, attended all the silver conferences and took an active, leading part in them. Senator Stewart let it be understood that he was a Populist, and he was treated as such by men of the party. Caucuses of Populists were frequently held in his committee-room in the Capitol Building and sometimes at his residence.

But, as plain matter of fact, Senator Stewart had at no time any sympathy with Populism. He was for silver and was always ready for a conference with men who favored silver, without regard to their party affiliations. When Populists approached him, asking his opinion as to what policy the party ought to agree upon with respect to the tariff question, he answered promptly, "Damn the tariff." He felt the same way, only he was a little more polite, if not so brief, in answering questions relating to every other subject put in issue by the Populist platform. He would not discuss land, transportation, referendum, or any other of the "isms" in the creed of the Populists, and which they treated as of vastly more importance.[7] On one occasion, in the Senate, when a Populist Senator had the floor and was asked a question by another Senator, Mr. Stewart asked permission to answer the question, and was refused

7. Stewart, in fact, had urged the reelection of Ingalls in 1891 in order to promote the silver cause and regarded the sacred Omaha Platform of the Populists as "so much trash." (See William M. Stewart to H. B. Kelly, January 23, 1891, and to Thomas Wren, July 8, 1892, in William M. Stewart Papers, Nevada State Historical Society, Reno.) Peffer's ardent commitment to a wide variety of social, political, and economic reforms was literally incomprehensible to the single-minded Stewart, who once attempted to ridicule the Kansan with these words: "We know Mr. Peffer well. He is an excellent man. His motives are pure and his patriotism unquestioned. The only difficulty with which he has to contend is obliquity of vision. All subjects and all objects appear to him of precisely the same importance and of the same size in every particular. He cannot possibly distinguish between a gnat and an elephant, nor can he see any difference between a cyclone and a zephyr. . . . He is in favor of reforming all things in all countries,

on the ground that "he had not been a Populist long enough to be an authority."

The *Congressional Directory* shows that Mr. Stewart was elected to the Senate in 1887 as a Republican, and that in 1893 he was re-elected, without even a suggestion that his party politics or party name had been changed. His radical views on silver accorded with public sentiment in his own State in 1892-93, and as the Populist was the only party that made an issue on silver, and in its favor, he naturally took its side in the silver fight.

But as soon as it became evident that the silver question had been taken up, or was about to be taken up, by the two great parties, Mr. Stewart insisted that Populists should abandon everything but the money question—just as General Weaver advised—and that, so far as Mr. Stewart was concerned, meant only restoration of unrestricted coinage of silver.

Senator Stewart was a leading spirit in the movement terminating in the formation of the American Bimetallic League and an attempt to form a bimetallic party. On March 5, 1895, a Washington dispatch announced: "The American Bimetallic League, which has been in progress here during the last two weeks, will soon issue an address to the American people asking their support for a new party having for the principal planks of its platform the free and unlimited coinage of silver at the ratio of 16 to 1 and a demand that the money of the country shall be issued by the government itself."

The dispatch announced further: "The address will inaugurate a new feature in American politics by doing away with the old system of nominating candidates. It will call upon the people themselves to nominate candidates for President and Vice President by petition. . . . The address will also place in nomination Joseph C.

whether great or small, at the same time, without stopping to take breath or giving his audience the slightest rest from his inexhaustible analysis of all things big and little" (*Silver Knight-National Watchman* [Washington, D.C.], August 26, 1897).

Sibley of Franklin, Pennsylvania, as a candidate for the Presidency."

Mr. Sibley is a well-known Democrat of Pennsylvania, who came into prominence through his honest and courageous opposition to monopolies in business and corruption in politics. He was popular in northwestern Pennsylvania, where, in 1892, he was nominated for Congress in a district adjoining the one he lived in. He was nominated by Democrats and indorsed by the Farmers' Alliance people and the Prohibitionists. He was elected by a large majority in a district strongly Republican.

Twenty-four States were reported to be represented in the conference which agreed upon this new departure. The address was issued in due time, assigning as a reason for inaugurating an independent movement that "Republicans and Democrats could not unite with Populists because the platform of that party contains declarations and the party advocates theories to which they cannot give their assent."

Mr. Sibley's candidacy was announced in a burst of enthusiasm, and he set out in a blaze of glory to capture the country.

The *New York World*, wishing to know and to inform its readers what Populists and silver Democrats thought of this new party movement, asked some of them to state their views on the subject, and on Sunday, March 31, 1895, published letters from them, introducing the correspondence in these words: "There is no longer a doubt that a determined effort is on foot to bring a new and formidable political party in the field for 1896. The beginning was made in the recent call issued from Washington by a number of 'free silver' Senators and Representatives for the formation of 'the American Bimetallic party.'"

Following are a few sentences from each of the letters, beginning with the Populists:

H. E. Taubeneck, Chairman of the Populist National Committee—"The People's party at its next national convention will declare in favor of making the money question the 'great central idea,' with no other plank except those which add strength to this one. Those who desire to retard monetary reform by loading us down with other issues will, with the Socialists and Communists, go to the rear."

Senator Butler, North Carolina—"They [silver Democrats and Republicans] would join the People's party, but they are to a greater or less extent prejudiced against some of the minor issues of that party. Financial reform and honest money have always been the overshadowing issue with the People's party, but the Populists (who always place reform and good government above party names and party ties) will join these honest money men from the old parties on this great question. Yes, the new party will come."

Thomas E. Watson, ex-Congressman from Georgia—"I do not believe there will be another political party formed by 1896, but I do believe that an understanding will [be] reached between the Populists, the American Bimetallic party, and the free silver elements of the Democratic and Republican parties which will amount practically to the formation of a united opposition to . . . (the gold standard party)."

General James B. Weaver—"In my judgment there will be an alliance—not fusion—formed between now and the opening of the campaign in 1896, made up of Populists, Democrats, and Republicans. It will first agree upon a platform, then declare its union perpetual until the objects in view are secured."

M. W. Howard,[8] Congressman from Alabama—"I do not think the voters in the People's party, of whom there are now over 2,000,000, are willing to abandon their fortifications and go over

8. Milford W. Howard of Fort Payne, Alabama, was a lawyer, author, and popular lecturer who first attracted attention in 1894 by writing a sensational book attacking Grover Cleveland and the Democratic Congress, *If Christ Came to Congress*, (Washington, D.C.: Howard Publishing Company, 1894). Alabama Populists twice elected him to Congress, where he attempted to impeach Cleveland and consistently supported Populist reform measures. He was a middle-of-the-road leader who opposed emphasizing silver to the neglect of other Populist principles and nominated Tom Watson for vice-president at the 1896 Populist National Convention.

bag and baggage into a silver party, the leaders of which will go back and affiliate with the two old parties the moment they secure the free coinage of silver."

Senator Peffer—"Yes, I do think a new party will be formed for 1896. But it will be built on a foundation broader and deeper than 'free silver' or 'bimetallism,' for these terms express nothing that reaches the core of the troubles which confront us."

From Democrats:

Senator Tillman[9]—"In my judgment, the organization of a new party is inevitable, and it will present as the main issue the restoration of bimetallism and the conduct of our finances in the interests of the people. The poverty and misery wrought by the fall of prices, directly traceable to the gold conspiracy and the contraction of the currency, will break up both the old parties—equally responsible for this crime against humanity—and cause a new alignment in politics."

A. J. Warner,[10] ex-Congressman and President of the American Bimetallic League—"That the silver question, or, more properly stated, the money question, is today the supreme issue in this coun-

9. Benjamin R. Tillman had been governor of South Carolina from 1890 to 1894 when he was elected to the first of four terms in the United States Senate. "Pitchfork Ben" Tillman appealed to rural Southern Democrats with his direct talk and promises of reform and he took the lead among Silver Democrats in attacking Cleveland, but he was essentially conservative and his lengthy domination of South Carolina politics produced little that was valuable or attractive. "You are the property of the old Conservative crowd," a disappointed former supporter told Tillman near the end of his career. Listing Tillman's acts of deception, corruption, fraud, and betrayal, he then referred to Pitchfork Ben's characteristically violent language: "You arrogantly invite anyone who doesn't like your black record to go to hell. Take care, you may meet them there" (quoted in Francis Butler Simkins, *Pitchfork Ben Tillman: South Carolinian* [Baton Rouge: Louisiana State University Press, 1944], 548).

10. Adoniram J. Warner of Marietta, Ohio, was four times elected to Congress as a Democrat between 1878 and 1886. In 1889 he helped organize the American Bimetallic League and thereafter was a leading figure in the silver lobby and a proponent of the new Silver party in 1895.

try can hardly be disputed, nor will the fact be questioned that on this issue lines are already clearly drawn. . . . The Democratic party will certainly split on this issue; it has already split; one part will go, or has gone, with the gold party, and the other cannot elect a President. The Republican party will also lose a score of Western States, besides votes by the hundred thousands in all the States. These States and these voters must get together if they would accomplish anything, and they will get together in the new party."

Joseph C. Sibley, candidate of American Bimetallic party for the Presidency—"A new party is already formed, with the money question as its chief issue. The active campaign will soon open, and no energy will be abated until the counted ballots of November, 1896, declare the will of the people. The party will be composed, not of Democrats, Republicans, and Populists, but of patriots who, for the time being, holding in abeyance all other issues upon which men divide into party organizations, will form a phalanx which at the proper time can strike a crushing blow against the organized rapacity of the international gold trust. The belief of the friends of bimetallism is that the cause will be lost or won before any of the Presidential conventions of 1896 have assembled."

The campaign which Mr. Sibley proposed to inaugurate so early and prosecute so vigorously and long, rounding up on election day a year and half hence, was duly opened by Mr. Sibley himself. He paused an hour or so during a splendid pyrotechnic display at Denver, then stepped over to the Pacific coast and dropped below the horizon.

VII
Democrats Corralling the Silver Forces

The Democrats whom the *World* asked for opinions touching the proposed new party did not pretend to speak for the party to which they belonged. General Warner had been several years at work on the silver question; Mr. Sibley was put out as a representative of the new movement; Senator Tillman expected a "new alignment of political forces," but had no clear ideas concerning the modus operandi of getting the lines formed.

The Democratic wheelhorses had and would have nothing whatever to do with the Sibley movement, only to watch it. The talk of the country was silver, but the Democratic managers never for a moment encouraged any independent movement on silver lines. The big silver conventions of 1895 were all engineered by trained partisans of the Democratic school. At Memphis, on June 13, 1895, a delegate convention of upward of 1,500 members, called by the Central Bimetallic League, reputed to be a non-partisan organization though managed by Democrats, met, and Senator Harris of Tennessee, a veteran Democrat and able man, was justly credited with having been the moving as well as the leading spirit of the occasion. When introducing Senator [David] Turpie of Indiana, another Democratic old-timer, as President of the convention, he gave warning in advance that nothing but the silver question was to be considered by the delegates.

"We are here," he said, "as a band of free men to consider this all-absorbing question which now confronts the American people. We are to consider the coinage question and that alone. That is the object of this convention, as I understand it, and as I believe it is understood by the hundreds of delegates here today."

On the platform when the convention was called to order were seated the following eminent Democrats: Senators Harris and Bate[1] of Tennessee, Senators Jones and Berry[2] of Arkansas, Senators George and Walthall of Mississippi,[3] Senator Turpie of Indiana; Governor Evans[4] of South Carolina, ex-Governor Prince[5] of New

1. William B. Bate had been a secessionist Democrat, Confederate general, and a Redeemer in turn. As a prominent Bourbon Democrat in the 1880s, he was elected first as governor, then as a United States Senator. His support for free silver did not extend to other agrarian reforms. He particularly opposed the subtreasury and regularly denounced Populists.

2. James H. Berry, a lawyer and former Arkansas governor, had first been elected to the Senate in 1885 and would serve until 1907.

3. Nothing convinced Peffer more of the deceptive and dangerous nature of the silver movement than the involvement in it of these two Mississippi Democratic Senators. James Z. George was a conservative Democrat who had been the chief organizer of the bloody overthrow of the Radical Republicans in Mississippi in 1875. Thereafter he was elected to the Senate in 1880, 1886, and 1892. A leading corporate lawyer, he strongly opposed the reform demands of the Farmers' Alliance, denouncing the subtreasury as "beyond the legitimate functions of the government," consistently attacked the Populists, and led the campaign for the notorious 1890 Mississippi constitutional convention to restrict popular suffrage. Not surprisingly, George also opposed monetary reform until he climbed on the silver bandwagon. Edward C. Walthall, a former Confederate general, was, like George, a conservative Democrat and corporate lawyer who served in the Senate from 1885 until 1898. Until 1894, Walthall had been a leading gold Democrat, but he switched to silver in order to preserve Democratic party harmony in Mississippi. Nevertheless, he affirmed his loyalty to the conservative Cleveland "in all but financial matters." For descriptions of both senators, see Albert D. Kirwan, *Revolt of the Rednecks: Mississippi Politics, 1876–1925* (Lexington: University of Kentucky Press, 1951), esp. 3, 48, 60–64, 86–88, 97.

4. John Gary Evans was a Tillman lieutenant who succeeded Pitchfork Ben as governor of South Carolina in 1894. In the same year that he promoted silver in the Memphis bimetallic convention, he urged the South Carolina constitutional convention to adopt suffrage restrictions.

Mexico, ex-Governor Eagle[6] of Arkansas, ex-Congressman Bryan[7] of Nebraska, General A. J. Warner of Ohio.

Among these distinguished Democrats was one Populist—Senator Marion Butler of North Carolina.

All the officers of the convention were Democrats. On the Committee on Resolutions there was not one Populist until Mr. McDowell[8] of Tennessee called attention to the fact, and requested that his party be represented on the committee. Senator Jones of Arkansas,

5. L. Bradford Prince, the governor of New Mexico Territory from 1889 to 1893, was in fact a Republican, but no more in accord with Peffer's views than the Southern Democrats sharing the Memphis platform. An attorney and mining speculator, Prince was a conservative on all issues except silver. He promoted fusion between Silver Republicans and Populists in New Mexico in 1896, but he refused to endorse the Populist platform and helped fracture the People's party in the territory.

6. James P. Eagle, one of the largest landowners in Arkansas, was a Bourbon Democrat who owed his 1888 election as governor to great fraud perpetrated against his Union Labor opponent.

7. William Jennings Bryan of Lincoln, Nebraska, was a liberal Democrat who had been elected to Congress in both 1890 and 1892 with Populist fusion help. After leaving Congress in early 1895, he took a prominent role in organizing Silver Democrats and became, of course, the presidential nominee of both Democrats and Populists in 1896.

8. John H. McDowell of Nashville, described by a contemporary as having a "mass of storm-stricken and insurrectionary whiskers [that] made him look like a weather-beaten tintype of Senator Peffer," was the controversial leader of Tennessee Populism. A former Democrat of some prominence, a superb orator, and the owner of the Nashville *Toiler*, he twice was elected state president of the Farmers' Alliance and helped organize the People's party in Tennessee in 1892, but his personal ambitions and expedient tactics frequently provoked bitter opposition. One Tennessee Populist editor, for example, denounced McDowell as "a moral coward, a spiteful villain, a treacherous wretch, a venomous reptile, and a voluminous liar. He has not even the vacuum where a conscience should be. The slime from his trail on earth will remain a stench in the nostrils of decency, and the fumes from his polluted heart will corrode the smokestacks of hell." (Quotations from Roger L. Hart, *Redeemers, Bourbons, and Populists: Tennessee, 1870–1896* [Baton Rouge: Louisiana State University Press, 1975], 169, 207.)

author of the so-called silver bill of the late session of Congress, was named first on the Resolutions committee. Congressman Money[9] began his speech by saying: "I am here as a silver man from head to foot and a Democrat all over." Private John Allen[10] of Mississippi provoked long and loud applause when in his speech he said that "the fight ought not to be taken outside the Democratic party."

Mr. Sibley spoke the night of the first day's session and ably and forcibly advocated an independent movement irrespective of party. Senator Tillman the second day, though speaking as a Democrat, expressed himself as ready for an independent party if it had [to] come to that; but his idea was that the silver men of his own party would soon be in the saddle and then silver men of other parties would come to them. Senators Stewart of Nevada and Butler of North Carolina both expressed a willingness to make common cause with the friends of silver in all parties.

This Memphis meeting was by all odds the most important political gathering of the year. Both sides of the new party question had able and earnest advocates, and they were heard with close and interested attention. But it was evident from the beginning that the convention was called by Democrats in the interest of the Democratic party, [and] the meeting was managed from start to finish by Democrats. The air was Democratic. Mr. Tillman said: "I speak as a Democrat in an assembly mostly Democratic."

The net result of the convention was to concentrate the silver

9. Hernando De Soto Money, a lawyer and editor, was a Democratic member of Congress from Mississippi from 1875 to 1885 and 1893 to 1897. Thereafter he was a senator from 1897 to 1911. An opponent of Populism, Money favored suffrage restriction in order to preserve Democratic hegemony in the South.

10. Private John Allen was a member of Congress from 1885 to 1901, and he compiled such an abysmal record that even many of his fellow Democrats denounced him. On the hustings, however, this "roguish clown" was in his element. For that characterization and an explanation of how Allen gained his nickname, see Kirwan, *Revolt of the Rednecks*, 106, 111–112.

sentiment among Democrats within the party in all parts of the country. A committee was appointed, toward the close of the meeting, consisting of one member from each State to correspond with the representatives and advocates of bimetallism and with officers of bimetallic associations in different sections of the country and to devise measures for advancing the cause throughout the United States. If any member of this important committee was not in accord with the spirit of the convention on the importance of "fighting it out within the party" the fact was not made known. The Memphis meeting was called for the purpose of sounding the alarm along the party lines, preparing the way for a movement to corral the silver forces of the country, and drive them into the Democratic camp.

The same strong partisan tendency of the silver movement was in evidence in the Senate at the beginning of the next session of Congress when Mr. Butler asked Senator Harris whether he had not received the notice of a conference among silver Senators for the purpose of considering the propriety of organizing the Senate on silver lines, and if he had received such notice why he did not attend.

Senator Harris answered:

> I did receive, I imagine, a copy of the paper the Senator reads, and the only remark I care to add is that up to this hour there has been no period of my life when I was willing to join in the organization of a great political party based upon one single idea. I have never been quite willing to organize a political party upon a single idea or a single proposition. Yet I am as earnest an advocate of the utilization of the free and unlimited coinage of silver as any one of the gentlemen who attached their names to that paper. (*Congressional Record* for December 30, 1895, vol. 28, part 1, page 425.)

VOL. XXXVI. No. 918.   PUCK BUILDING, New York, October 10th, 1894.   PRICE 10 CENTS.
Copyright, 1894, by Keppler & Schwarzmann.

Entered at N. Y. P. O. as Second-class Mail Matter.

PEFFER'S POPULISTIC BOOM.

A collapsing Populist party was a frequent theme and fervent hope of conservative cartoonists. This drawing reflects the wishful thinking among Democrats on the eve of the 1894 elections. (Puck, October 10, 1894)

Senator Butler was the youngest member of the Senate, and as he afterwards became Chairman of the National Executive Committee of the People's Party, it will be of interest to know something of his history, and what he thought of the Democratic party at and before the time when his question brought out the above quoted answer from Senator Harris.

Mr. Butler is an educated man, having graduated in his twenty-second year at the University of North Carolina in 1885. He began the study of law, but by reason of the death of his father he was called home to manage the farm. He taught at a neighboring academy several years. In 1888 he joined the Farmers' Alliance and bought the *Clinton Caucasian*, a weekly newspaper, which was afterwards conducted in the interest of the Alliance. He was elected to the State Senate in 1890, and was recognized as the leader of the Alliance forces in that body and worked on reform lines. He was elected President of the State Farmers' Alliance in 1891, and was reelected the next year. In 1893, he was elected Vice President of the National Farmers' Alliance and Industrial Union, and one year later he was chosen President of that body, succeeding Colonel L. L. Polk, deceased. Immediately after the adjournment of the National Democratic convention at Chicago in 1892 Mr. Butler severed his connection with the Democratic party and took an active and leading part in building up the People's Party in his State; and in the winter of 1893-'94 he conceived the plan of campaign which resulted in such a triumphant success at the fall election of 1894. He was Chairman of the Populist State Committee during that campaign. His paper, the *Caucasian*, was moved to Raleigh and was a power among the Populists. Through a union of Populists and Republicans in the election campaign of 1894 and subsequently in the State Legislature, Mr. Butler, Populist, and J. C. Pritchard,[11]

11. Jeter C. Pritchard was the leading Republican in western North Carolina. Elected three times to the state legislature during the 1880s, he favored fusion with the Populists in the 1890s as a tactic to defeat the Democrats. As Pritchard was committed to the gold standard and a high

Republican, were elected to the United States Senate—Butler for the full term of six years, beginning March 4, 1895; Pritchard for the remainder of the unexpired term of Mr. Vance,[12] deceased, ending March 3, 1897.

In the colloquy between Senators Butler and Harris over the refusal of the latter to attend the conference proposed by Populists to reorganize the Senate in the interest of silver, something was said about mixing politics, and the record shows the following:

> Mr. Harris—Will the Senator allow me to ask him a question?
>
> Mr. Butler—You may.
>
> Mr. Harris—The Senator speaks of combining with other organizations. I hope it is not impertinent if I ask the Senator if he does not hold the seat he occupies upon this floor by a combination between the Populists and the Republicans of the State that he in part represents?
>
> Mr. Butler—I will answer the question with pleasure. I hold my seat by such a cooperation for the simple reason that the party in my State which you belong to got to be so corrupt the people in the State rebelled against its management. Your party could today be in full power in North Carolina if it had stood by its pledges and promises. A cooperation of all who opposed its methods was made, but that combination could not have driven the Democratic party from power in North Carolina if that party had been true to its pledges, true to its promises, and true to its people. It not only deserted the principles of Thomas Jefferson and Andrew Jackson, thereby dis-

tariff, his election to the Senate in 1895, and his reelection to a full term in 1897, illustrated the limitations of the fusion arrangements devised by Butler.

12. Zebulon B. Vance had been a Democratic member of Congress in the 1850s, governor of North Carolina during the Civil War and again from 1876 to 1878, and United States Senator from 1879 until his death in 1894.

gusting the great rank and file of the party, but it tried to keep itself in power by stealing and perjury at the ballot box, by ballot-box stuffing and manipulating the returns. This made fair elections—the purity of the ballot box—the overshadowing issue in North Carolina politics. A large majority of the voters of the State joined in a movement to correct these abuses. The Democratic party held the election machinery and under a vicious election law determined to count enough votes in the last election to keep them in power. But the revolt of the people against the Democratic machine was greater than the leaders anticipated. They stole over 30,000 votes, but fell 20,000 short of having enough. Yes, we freed North Carolina, and, I trust, forever, from such corrupt methods. This was done with the help of men who had been Democrats all their lives. I trust that I have given the Senator from Tennessee a full and satisfactory answer to his question.

Senator Butler then resumed his speech condemning Democrats, especially, for not attending and taking part in the proposed conference looking to the silver men, as such, taking charge of the Senate, reorganizing the committees, and the official force on silver lines. He said: "Mr. President, we (meaning the Populist Senators who had called the conference and attended it) were sorely disappointed, and on top of it we see interviews in the newspapers from gentlemen on the other side (meaning Democratic Senators) saying the country will go to perdition if we do not have free coinage, and yet, in the same interviews, saying that if their party nominates a gold bug for President next time they will bow down and lick his feet and vote for him."

Continuing, Mr. Butler said:

There is something I wish to say now, and say with emphasis. I would not say it, for I dislike to say unpleasant things, but for the fact that I believe the situation in this country is so perilous with respect to the welfare of the people that I ought to say it. It is this: Free coinage would have been secured long ago if it had not been for those who claim to be free coinage men, but who sacrifice it for party success. If these men would stand for free coinage, party or no party, the people of this country would have had free coinage before now. It is the men who talk free coinage in campaigns, but bow to the party lash in their national conventions, where gold bugs, who have prevented the passage of free coinage legislation, tell them which way to vote. Such men are the worst enemies of free coinage, although they profess to be its friends. . . . There is something else. I do not think the members of the party which the Senator from Tennessee [Mr. Harris] represents can afford to ask for Populist help so long as they stay inside of that party with its present views and leadership. I wish to say that, in my humble opinion, his party does not deserve the support or help of the People's Party. It had a majority in the last Congress, and yet on the statute books today there is a Republican law giving the President power to issue bonds. He issued bonds under your teeth here in the last Congress. And we understand now that he is in another dark lantern trade, negotiating with private individuals for the sale of more bonds under a law that the Democratic party has denounced but refused to repeal when it had the power. We suppose the President will make another deal that will put millions of the people's money into private pockets. The People's Party is opposed to such infamous laws and to such infamous transactions. Therefore, the Democratic party does not deserve Populist support any more than the Republican party, on its record, deserves Populist support, and neither party will get it.

The particular point which Senator Butler had in mind when he used the language last above quoted, was the supposition and the expectation on the part of Democratic Senators that, notwithstanding their refusal to attend the conference and try to arrange for action on common ground (silver) in reorganizing the Senate, they, the Democrats, had some sort of claim on Populist support in reorganizing on Democratic lines. When the time to vote on reorganization came, Populists were present to make a quorum, but declined to vote on nominations, leaving the two old parties to settle the matter between them; and, as to them, Republicans had a majority and won. The Populist Senators did not feel like kissing the hand that smote them.

VIII
Absorption of the
National Watchman

[NOTE—The author of these articles was so closely and intimately identified with the Populist movement and his public record is so interwoven with the birth and career of the People's Party that it is impossible to write its history without occasionally referring and alluding to him, and that is the best and only excuse I have to offer for offending in this particular.—THE AUTHOR.]

In the winter of 1891–'92, during the early part of the first session of the Fifty-second Congress, after it had become evident that the Southern Alliance members would not affiliate with the Northern independents and Populists, and that, therefore, the *National Economist*, Dr. Macune's paper, could not be relied on to support the new People's Party movement, the Northern men, with Watson of Georgia, undertook to establish a representative party paper of their own. A corporation, capitalized at $10,000, was formed under the laws of the District of Columbia, with Senator Peffer as President. The new paper was named the *National Watchman*, and Mr. N. A. Dunning was employed as editor.[1] Mr. Dun-

1. Nelson A. Dunning of Sykesville, Maryland, was the author of *The Farmers' Alliance History and Agricultural Digest* (Washington, D.C.: Alliance Publishing Company, 1891) and the state chair of the People's party in Maryland.

ning had been some time associated with Dr. Macune in the editorial work of the *Economist*, which, as the reader will remember, was established and conducted by Mr. Macune as the national representative of the Farmers' Alliance and Industrial Union.

Mr. Macune himself was a Democrat, so born and reared, and his feelings being in accord with his party prejudices he was opposed to the new party policy, and his paper bore unmistakable evidence that its editor knew well how to say both politely and clearly what he desired in this respect. If the Alliance could be kept within the Democratic party there would be no immediate danger to the party, the Alliance, or the *National Economist*.

Dunning, on the other hand, had been a Republican, and he was in favor of the Populist movement. He had been long enough with the *Economist* to be well versed in Alliance literature; he was well informed generally; was a ready writer and brim full of energy. Dunning was as much opposed to hybridizing Populism with Democracy as Macune was to divorcing the Farmers' Alliance from the Democratic party.

The *Watchman* soon began to circulate widely. It went into every State and Territory—so the editor once reported. It grew with the party, and if the fusion fever had not crazed many Populists the *National Watchman* could and probably would have become a permanent power for good in the country. But, alas! alas! Dunning thought he saw evidences of fusion in Nebraska, and the *Watchman* by referring to the matter in unfriendly terms—advising against all dickering with other parties—and accusing Senator Allen and Congressmen Kem and McKeighan with encouraging it offended those gentlemen. They demanded a retraction on the part of the paper, but the editor refused to do anything more than to permit them to use the columns of the *Watchman* in making any statement which they thought the circumstances warranted or required. That was not satisfactory to them, and, of course, the paper lost their good will.

It perhaps ought to be stated here, in justice to all parties, that the President of the Watchman Publishing Company was appealed to and he sustained the editor—not because of any opinion he held as to the correctness of the editor's original charge, but as to his way of treating the demand for retraction.

Whether Dunning was right or wrong in his first impressions, it is clear that Nebraska soon became prolific in her fusion offspring. The *Congressional Directory* for the Fifty-third Congress shows that Mr. McKeighan "was nominated for Congress by the Alliance or Independent party, was indorsed by the Democratic convention, and elected to the Fifty-second and reelected to the Fifty-third Congress as an independent, receiving 17,400 votes, against 14,230 votes for William E. Andrews, Republican, and 838 votes for O. C. Hubbell, People's party." (*Congressional Directory*, third session, Fifty-third Congress, page 71.)

The directory for the second session, Fifty-fourth Congress, shows that Mr. Kem "was elected to the Fifty-fourth Congress as a Populist, receiving 17,077 votes, against 14,676 votes for Matthew Dougherty, Republican, and 891 votes for Bone, Prohibitionist." There was no Democratic opposition to Mr. Kem's election. He received every Democratic vote cast for Congressman. At the same election, November, 1894, Silas A. Holcomb,[2] classified as Demo-Populist, received 97,815 votes, to 94,815 for Mr. Majors, Republican, and 6,985 votes for Sturdevant, Silver-Democrat. Governor Holcomb received the almost unanimous vote of the Democratic party and was elected by and only by the aid of that vote.

It appears from these records that Editor Dunning was not far

2. Silas A. Holcomb, a former Democrat and a district judge, had been the unsuccessful Populist candidate for the Nebraska Supreme Court in 1893. Following his 1894 gubernatorial nomination by the Populists, William Jennings Bryan nominated him in the Democratic state convention. The Democrats followed Bryan's advice and endorsed Holcomb, although a splinter group of conservative Cleveland Democrats did run a separate ticket that attracted few votes. As governor, Holcomb was criticized by many Populists for too generously rewarding his Democratic supporters through patronage and policy concessions, and he became a prominent advocate of Bryan's presidential candidacy in 1896.

out of the way when he called "fusion" in Nebraska in 1895. However, the *Watchman's* offending lay rather in another direction—that of interfering in the politics of the State. It was claimed that the national party paper had no business meddling with local politics anywhere. But the *Watchman* kept hammering away at fusion, trying to keep the People's Party from mixing with others and thus endangering its future standing before the country. Correspondents began to write to the editor asking for advice on the general subject of fusion with the new silver party and the *Watchman* told them to let the silver movement alone, that the Populist was a silver party, the first and only one then on the map, and counseled Populists to keep their wits about them and support their own colors.

Naturally the *Watchman* people were uneasy at the prospect of the paper's friends and supporters being swept off their feet by the silver tide. The President of the company prepared a letter on the subject addressed to the editor of the *Watchman*. It was printed in the spring of 1895 in the *Watchman*, beginning as follows: "There are breakers ahead. Does the *Watchman* see them and is it steering safely?"

The letter was long, touching on all the irritating spots, concluding thus:

> In conclusion, . . . permit me to say that the *Watchman* was established by Populists to aid them in their party work. We look to it for leadership and for counsel. We expect to rely largely on its foresight and advice. And now, more than ever, we need the benefit of its careful watching. Political elements are in commotion. The air is full of projects to form new parties, and all because of the principles advocated by us. One has already been collected on a plank in our platform, and some of our people are asking you what they ought to do about it. Your advice could not have been better—simply to observe the 'let alone' policy. This new silver party in its first official utterance took occasion to say that its members could not support our principles. That relieves us of all responsibility in the matter. Why should we go outside our own party to

support our own measures, and especially when we are informed in advance that before we would be accepted as recruits in the other camp we must remove our uniform? Ours is
the only party that advocates the free and unlimited coinage
of gold and silver at the present ratio. And that is all there is
in this silver movement. Let the silver party go ahead in its
own way. Whatever good it accomplishes will be that much
gain for the country. But the good body of silver Democrats
and Republicans will insist on remaining with their own parties in the hope of capturing their national conventions. That
will precipitate a condition of things greatly in the public interest if the Populists keep their heads and stand by their
guns.

I expect to see a great party rise in the future and sweep
over the country like a tidal wave; but it will form itself
around the banner of Populism. Our doctrines reach the dis-
ease from which the country suffers; our declarations are responsive to the people's needs. Let us stand by them, teach
them, and vote them.

A newspaper organ was needed to represent the new movement,
and the *Silver Knight* was started by Senator Stewart, to be published in Washington City. The Senator was rich enough to send out
50,000 or 100,000 copies gratuitously if he so desired. The *Silver
Knight* took well from the start; it was something new, [it had] a
catching name, and besides it was floating on the flowing silver
tide. Its circulation cut into that of the *Watchman*. The *Knight's*
editor appealed to Populists for support and solicited correspondence from prominent members of the party.

One day (October 10, 1895) the *Silver Knight* contained an editorial article on the duty of Populists, arguing that they ought to drop
everything but the money question and make the fight for silver in
that way, and the editor asked different persons, among them the
Populist Senator from Kansas, to write out what they thought about

the proposition and let him print their views in his paper. Here are a
few extracts from Mr. Peffer's answer, dated October 21, 1895:

> The *Silver Knight* would cut down our platform to a single
> issue of "monetary reform." It concedes that ours is the only
> party which advocates monetary reform, and truthfully says
> "it is much easier to utilize a great party like the Populist
> party than to create a new one"; but, because our platform
> contains provisions that the *Knight* does not approve, it
> doubts whether this most desirable union can be brought
> about. . . . The obstacles which the *Silver Knight* thinks it
> sees in the way of a union with us, which it so earnestly and
> wisely desires, are largely imaginary and can be easily over-
> come. The Omaha platform was prepared and adopted under
> peculiar circumstances. It was made by men representing
> many different bodies that had never worked together and
> that held different views concerning the sources from which
> our common troubles arose, and every one of them properly
> took part in the work of constructing the new party platform.
> The wonder is that so good a piece of work was done. Look-
> ing back at it from this distance, we can all see where it could
> have been improved if we had then had the light we have now.
> Its phraseology might have been so put as to bring out more
> clearly and with less offense the leading principles involved.
> Some expressions could have been omitted because their sub-
> stance is included in other sentences. I believe that a single
> paragraph can now be prepared that will clearly set forth the
> great principle of popular rights underlying the Populist
> creed; that its application to all the great departments of in-
> dustry and government can be well stated in three or four
> planks of a platform; and that this can be done so as to add
> to the force of every vital proposition and yet get rid of read-
> ing to which some even of our own members object, leaving
> the document one in which every sincere reformer will find
> the germ of his own belief. . . . All things considered, there is

really nothing insurmountable in the *Silver Knight's* objections. On all the essentials of monetary reform it is in full accord with us. Its proper place is in our ranks. Every "silver man" ought to be fighting with us, for even if we had free silver coinage and nothing else, we should be no better off than we are now.

The *Silver Knight*, though its editor and proprietor was looked on at that time quite generally as a Populist, was exerting all its influence to neutralize everything in the Populist creed not centering in silver. The *Silver Knight* had the moral support of all silver Democrats and the financial support of a great many of them. It invaded Populist communities and undermined the prestige and influence of the *National Watchman*. It demoralized Populists and led them away from their colors. It held up the silver image and bade its Populist readers to forsake everything else in their platform which they regarded as fundamental and worship that—the image.

Finally, the *Watchman* had to give way. Mr. Dunning tried hard and faithfully to save it, and when he found that it had to go under he hoped to get it into strictly Populist hands. He made several suggestions to the President of the company in efforts to persuade him to take charge of the paper, but he did not feel able to lose any more money in the wreck than he had already invested. So the *National Watchman*, established by Populists to help build up their party and to become a useful instrument for good, was sold to Senator Stewart and was absorbed in the *Silver Knight* before the great campaign of 1896 had opened; and Democracy got a clear field for their own newspaper work. There is no better Democratic paper in the country than the *Silver Knight-Watchman*, with Senator William M. Stewart as managing editor.

IX
Democracy Captures the Populist Vote

As if enough had not already been said to make it clear to everybody in and about the national capital that Democratic and Republican champions of silver had no use for anything that Populists had, except their votes, Senator Dubois of Idaho, in a speech delivered on January 23, 1896, added his testimony. The following extracts are taken from the record of that day's proceedings. (See vol. 28, *Congressional Record*, part 1, p. 906.) Mr. Dubois said:

The Populist Senators have had considerable to say during this session on financial and other subjects, and I heartily subscribe to many of their utterances. There seems to be, however, a concerted movement on their part to place Senators in the Democratic and Republican parties who are, and have always been, able and fearless advocates of the full and complete restoration of silver in the position of being untrue to silver unless they blindly indorse Populistic doctrines and methods. For the time being they are keeping the real aims and policies of their party in the background, so far as they can, and are posing here as the especial friends and advocates of silver. The junior Senator from North Carolina [Mr. Butler] called attention to a circular letter addressed to the advocates of silver coinage which was issued at the beginning of this Congress, and argued from the fact that the Democratic and Republican believers in free coinage did not attend this meeting that they were not genuine silver advocates. I will quote from the *Congressional Record* of December 30, 1895, page 428.

The Senator read the note addressed by Populist Senators to the silver members of the Senate inviting them to a conference with the view of uniting in the reorganization of the Senate on silver lines. Mr. Dubois then proceeded:

I was the recipient of a similar invitation, as well as were all real and supposed silver Senators. I am informed that two or three silver advocates responded to the call, merely to protest against the policy suggested in the circular. Nothing in the interest of silver could have been accomplished if the program of the Populists had been carried out. Silver interests, so far as the Senate committees are concerned, are in the Finance Committee. Under the organization which has been consummated, or under any organization which would have been allowed, the silver sentiment predominates. . . . The Senate does not depend, fortunately, on the Populist vote for its silver strength. It is not necessary, luckily, in order to gain votes for silver, that we indorse Populistic ideas in general. The Populists in the Senate will vote for the [Jones] bill under consideration, and for any free coinage bill, and true silver men, regardless of party, are pleased to have their votes. They do not vote for the unlimited coinage of silver, however, because they believe that silver should be basic money.

They want more money. They do not believe in basic money of ultimate redemption. Their theory is that the Government by its fiat can make money, and that it should do so, the amount of the money thus created to depend on the will of the people as expressed by its representatives in Congress. The hard money men, who constitute a majority in this chamber—this majority made up of Democrats and Republicans—

believe that gold and silver should form the basis of our currency and that all forms of money should rest on those two metals, and that they should be the money of ultimate redemption.

Our argument is that there is not enough of gold to form a safe and adequate basis, and that the basis should be broadened by restoring silver. Our Populist friends care for neither gold nor silver and would discard both and have the government issue paper money which is redeemable in itself. I call attention to a debate in the Senate during the debate on the repeal of the Sherman act, which clearly defines their position. It will be found in the *Congressional Record* of October 28, 1893, page 2,923.

This refers to an amendment proposed by Mr. Peffer to issue $250,000,000 in Treasury notes, redeemable in lawful money.

Mr. Dubois continued:

Mr. President, a vote was had on the amendment of the Senator from Kansas, and on the roll call the amendment secured seven votes, the other Senators, fifty-eight in number, voting against it. Every Populist Senator voted for it. . . . Nothing could more clearly demonstrate the views of the Populist party on the money question than this amendment, debate, and vote. It is strictly in accord with their national platform. . . . The Senator from North Carolina [Mr. Butler] was not here when this position was taken by his party on the amendment of the Senator from Kansas [Mr. Peffer]; but, no doubt, he would subscribe to the doctrine of his party as then announced. Within the last few days the Senator from Nebraska [Mr. Allen], who is, without doubt, the best exponent of the principles of his party in this Chamber, stated his belief that the Government should own and operate the Pacific railroads, if not all railroads. The doctrine also is incorporated in their national platform. I do not subscribe to it and will not support it. . . . Then, again, the Populists are free traders if they are anything on the question of the tariff. Every member of their party in the House voted for the Wilson bill, which was as nearly a free trade measure as could be passed. The Senator from Kansas, Mr. Peffer, voted against the amended Wilson bill in the Senate, but their party and party platform are favorable to free trade. . . . The reasons given are sufficient to explain why the silver Republicans did not join with the Populists. There is no sympathy between us.

Senator Dubois was the youngest of the silver Senators on the Republican side, and by common consent he was taken as the best steering committeeman they had. His statements along the line which divided silver Republicans from Populists may be taken as given by authority of his associates.

Senator Harris was the oldest among the Democratic silver Senators, and he was looked on among his associates as properly entitled, by reason of special fitness, discarding age, to take the lead in the matter of concentrating the silver vote. He had expressed himself, in answer to Senator Butler, plainly, stating why he did not attend the conference proposed by Populists; and though he did not assume to speak for other Democratic Senators, he may be presumed to have satisfied them, for none of them spoke for themselves.

Senator Harris charged that Populists had but one idea—silver coinage—and he could not entertain a proposition to join in a political movement where only a single idea was involved. Senator Dubois gave, as his reasons for not attending the conference, that the Populists had several ideas, with none of which he and his associates had any sympathy.

Still, notwithstanding this two-edged rebuff and reproof, the Populist members of both Houses went into conference among themselves, and appointed a committee to confer with Dubois and his associates on the Republican side, and with Senator Jones [of Arkansas] and his associates on the Democratic side, as to the best means of uniting the silver forces for the campaign of 1896 in opposition to the Republican party.

The Populist contingent in Congress at that time consisted of six Senators—Allen of Nebraska, Jones and Stewart of Nevada, Butler of North Carolina, Kyle of South Dakota, and Peffer of Kansas—and seven members of the House—Howard of Alabama, Bell of Colorado, Baker of Kansas, Kem of Nebraska, and Skinner,[1] Strowd,[2] and Shuford[3] of North Carolina—thirteen in all.

These met frequently in conference to discuss plans of the campaign then approaching. It soon developed that the errand of General Weaver to Washington in February the year before, and the publication of the manifesto he took with him, had been fruitful, for eleven of these thirteen Populists in Congress were in favor of forming an alliance with the Democrats in the campaign. The other two—Howard of Alabama and Peffer of Kansas—were opposed to any kind of an alliance or union with any other party, or of cooperating with any other organization. They argued that a movement of that character would eventually work the ruin of the Populist party

1. Harry Skinner of Pitt County, North Carolina, had been a Democratic state legislator and party official until 1892 when he joined the People's party, his decision prompted in large measure by the Democratic rejection of the subtreasury, a concept that Skinner energetically championed. He was elected to Congress in 1894 and 1896. Of moderate mid-road sympathies, he later broke from Marion Butler, whose fusionist policies Skinner believed "caused our party to be a harlot between the old parties" (quoted in Eric Anderson, *Race and Politics in North Carolina, 1872-1901: The Black Second* [Baton Rouge: Louisiana State University Press, 1981], 233).

2. William F. Strowd, a farmer of Chatham County, North Carolina, was an unsuccessful Populist nominee for Congress in 1892, but he was elected in both 1894 and 1896.

3. Alonzo C. Shuford was an early organizer and lecturer for the Farmers' Alliance. A frequent delegate to the several reform conventions of the early 1890s, including the Omaha Convention of the People's party in 1892, he was elected to Congress as a Populist in both 1894 and 1896. In 1924 Shuford was a presidential elector on the ticket of La Follette and Wheeler.

and delay if not utterly submerge every reform urged by the party. They held that the People's Party was formed on new and vital issues distinct and apart from those advocated by other parties and wholly unlike them, and that even temporarily to join with another party holding views antagonistic to our own would lower our standard, remove from the field of discussion our leading ideas, and place ourselves before the world as men without confidence in themselves or faith in their creed, thereby bringing disrespect on the party and shame on its supporters.

The success of the Democratic silver work in '95 satisfied the leaders that the silver wing of the party would be able to control the national convention, and in that event it was understood that free coinage and an income tax would be incorporated in the party platform to secure the Populist vote.

The great body of the Populists in all parts of the country favored an early convention of the party that their doctrines, declarations, and candidates might be announced before any of the other party conventions had been held. The demand for an early convention was quite general, and, up to that time, there was no expectation of a postponement and no desire was expressed anywhere that such a course should be pursued. Populist papers generally had agreed on May as a proper month for the convention; some of them had announced their preference of candidates for nomination for the Presidency; and some had opened voting contests for candidates.

About the middle of January, 1896, the Populist National Executive Committee was in session in St. Louis for the purpose of fixing the time and place for holding the national convention and arranging the details. At a Populist conference in Washington it was determined, after long and animated debate, to wire a message to the committee at St. Louis advising a late date for the convention. Mr. Peffer, being in the minority in the conference, and being the first distinctively Populist Senator ever chosen, was requested to first attach his name to the message. This he declined to do, but, expressing his disapproval of the whole proceeding and declaring it

*Despite Peffer's increasing isolation in the Populist party as it drifted toward silver politics and fusion, cartoonists continued to depict him as a possible presidential nominee. Here he joins Benjamin Harrison, John Sherman, and other leading politicians in steering toward the prize. (*Puck, *June 12, 1895)*

as his belief that the party would ultimately lose itself in the Democracy, [he] joined the others present in the message.

Senator Butler favored a late convention. He went to St. Louis, and attended the meeting of the committee for the purpose of urging that course; and this message from his associates at Washington greatly strengthened his efforts. The time fixed for holding the convention was July 22—two weeks after the date of opening the National Democratic convention, and the Republicans had adjourned a week before that event happened.

This proceeding handcuffed the party. It was placed at the mercy of trained politicians, and from that time forward the majority members of the Washington managers were in frequent conference with the Democratic majority arranging for the handling of the

Chicago [Democratic] convention. The effect on the Populist voters was discouraging, and protests went up from all directions. Not one among the leading and influential papers of the party approved the policy of delay. But the best was made of what then appeared to be only a mistake of judgment rather than a scheme deliberately planned to consolidate the Populist vote of the country with that of the Democracy and silver Republicans.

When the time came for holding the Democratic convention, July 7, the Chairman of the Populist National Committee, Mr. Taubeneck, and several other members of the committee attended and assisted as best they could in shaping things so as to be as little as possible distasteful to Populist voters. Senator Dubois was there also, with several other silver Republicans of more or less prominence.

When the [Democratic] platform was announced, so far the outlook was encouraging, but it was generally expected that Mr. Bland or some other Democrat of the old school would be named as the party's candidate for the Presidency, and that would not have been acceptable to many members of the People's party.[4] Mr. Bland's prospect was so encouraging to his friends that he was regarded as a "sure winner," having at least 400 votes to begin with.

Populists present were frightened at the outlook. Twenty-nine of them got together at the Briggs House, with Chairman Taubeneck in the lead, and drew up a manifesto, reminding the Democratic delegates that the People's Party was already in the field for silver; that it began business four years before; that it had other issues be-

---

4. Richard P. Bland of Missouri had been a Democratic member of the House of Representatives from 1873 until 1895. He was closely associated with the silver movement, having given his name to the Bland-Allison Act of 1878, which revived limited silver coinage, and having framed (with William Jennings Bryan) the 1895 "Appeal of the Silver Democrats," which advocated free silver and the reorganization of the Democratic party on that basis. "Silver Dick" worked closely with the American Bimetallic League but rejected the suggestion of leaving the Democratic party to achieve free silver. Moreover, despite some liberal inclinations, Bland—unlike Bryan—had not cooperated with the Populists in state politics and had little support among them.

sides silver; that it had as many votes in the States that were sure for silver as the Democratic had all told, where its vote in the gold States was eliminated; that it was unreasonable to expect a party as big as this, with silver now in its platform, to vote for any Democrat as its candidate for the Presidency; that if this convention expected the support of the Populists it must put up a man acceptable to them, and that they thought Senator Teller, as the Democratic candidate on a free coinage platform, would unite the Populist and silver Republican vote solidly.[5]

This manifesto was published immediately, and although it was signed by the Chairman of the National Populist Committee, by General Weaver, the party's candidate for President in 1892, and by several other Populists of distinction, the delegates laughed at it. They said they were running a Democratic convention, they would adopt a Democratic platform with a free coinage plank in it, then name a Democrat as their candidate, and if Populists were sincere in their advocacy of silver they would support such a platform and such a candidate. The Teller bubble burst and the Populist meddlers had learned what they ought to have known in the beginning—that when any wing of a nominating convention has a majority it invariably puts up one of its own men.

When the news spread that Mr. Bryan of Nebraska, a young man of the new school, had been nominated, Western Populists were swept off their feet, and when they had time to catch breath, they thought and they said, with wonderful and spontaneous unanimity, that the best thing to be done under the circumstances was to make the Nebraskan their candidate. Among answers to questions of newspaper men about the feeling of the delegates the fol-

5. Henry M. Teller, a veteran Republican Senator from Colorado, had bolted the 1896 Republican National Convention when it had adopted a "sound money" plank. With other Western Republicans he then formed the Silver Republican party, which urged all who favored bimetallism to unite behind Teller as the common silver presidential candidate against the Republican nominee William McKinley.

lowing appeared in the *New York Journal* the morning of the first day of the [Populist] convention [in St. Louis]:

"If this convention should refuse to indorse Bryan, the Populist party would not contain a handful of men in November."
JERRY SIMPSON

Senator Butler was voted into the temporary chairmanship by the friends of Mr. Bryan. Before taking the chair Mr. Butler, among other things, was reported to have said:

They (the Populists) had at last torn the mask from the old parties. A few weeks ago the Republican party had been forced to align itself with the money kings of Wall street and Europe. The Democratic party at Chicago was driven to the alternative of siding with gold or with the people. They were so frightened that in their desperation they finally committed grand and petty larceny. They stole our platform and tried to steal our party. If the People's party should abandon its organization, the Democratic party, at its next national convention, would repudiate the platform adopted at Chicago and Bryan would not have any more chance of being nominated than Thomas Jefferson would if he were alive today.

Senator Allen was made permanent Chairman by the Bryan vote. Bryan men had charge of the convention, but it required two pledges from them before a bolt could be prevented. They had to agree, first, to allow the antis to name the candidate for Vice President; and, second, to take the vote on Vice President before that for the head of the ticket. This arrangement brought about the following correspondence by telegraph:

St. Louis, Mo., July 24, 1896.—To W.J. Bryan, Lincoln, Neb.: The Populists will nominate Vice President first. If not

Sewall[6], what shall we do? I favor your declination in that case. Answer quick. JAMES K. JONES, Chairman Democratic National Committee.

Within an hour this answer came:

Lincoln, Neb., July 24, 1896.—To Senator J.K. Jones, Chairman National Committee, St. Louis: I entirely agree with you. Withdraw my name if Sewall is not nominated. W.J. BRYAN.

Governor Stone of Missouri[7] conveyed the answer of Mr. Bryan to convention hall and showed it to Chairman Allen, but it was not made public then, although its contents soon spread among the delegates, and there were urgent demands among Southern delegates for the reading of the dispatch.

The vote on Vice President was:

Watson, Populist 561
Sewall, Democrat 256

6. Arthur M. Sewall, a Maine banker and shipbuilder, had received the Democratic nomination for vice-president. Although Sewall favored free silver, he was otherwise denounced as "plutocratic" by most Populists. Peffer early suggested replacing Sewall with a Southern Populist, and others quickly endorsed the idea as a means of preserving the separate identity of the People's party, mollifying Southern Populists dismayed at the prospect of fusing with the Democrats on Bryan, and still substantially maintaining a unity of the silver forces.

7. A Democratic member of Congress from 1885 to 1891 and governor of Missouri from 1893 to 1897, William J. Stone was a leading Silver Democrat. In 1895 he helped organize the Democratic National Bimetallic Committee and then served on its executive committee. A close associate of Bryan's and influential in the 1896 Democratic National Convention, Stone was then named to both the party's notification committee and its national executive committee. Beginning in 1903, he was elected to three terms in the United States Senate.

Changes were made from other candidates voted for, raising Watson's vote to 721. Necessary to a choice, 699.

The vote on President stood:

> Bryan 1,042
> Norton[8] 321
> Scattering 10

The feeling among anti-Bryan delegates was intense, more especially those from Georgia and Texas, and a movement was begun to demand [of the Democratic party] the withdrawal of Sewall and the substitution of Watson, but the convention, having adopted a platform and provided for the appointment of a National Committee, consisting of three members from each State, with the powers of the convention itself—to do anything that the appointing body might do—adjourned sine die.

8. Seymour F. Norton was a former Greenbacker and the Populist editor of the *Chicago Sentinel*. A leading opponent of free silver as a monetary panacea, he was the author of the widely circulated *Ten Men of Money Island*, an 1891 Populist pamphlet restating Greenback doctrine. Norton was a member of the platform committee of the 1891 Cincinnati Conference and a featured speaker at the 1892 Omaha Convention, but in 1896 he was the candidate of the mid-road Populist delegates only after they were unable to persuade Peffer or any other more prominent politician to stand for the nomination.

X
Effect of the Fusion Movement of 1896

The effect of the fusion movement of 1896 was (1) to divide the Populist party, (2) to prevent a reunion of the Populist voters, and (3) to merge a large number of Populists in the national Democracy.

A great many details of the campaign necessarily had to be left to the National Committee operating through local officers. The party organization had to be retained and a party platform adopted or there could have been no such thing as making a Democrat the party nominee. While, as the vote on Vice President showed, about one-fourth part of the delegates in the national convention were then ready to join the Democracy in a body the other three-fourths were not so ready, and this tampering with another party while retaining the regular party machinery rendered it impracticable to avoid friction between the parties in localities where there was a disposition on the part of Democrats to manage the Populists' part of the campaign work. At least 75 per cent of the members of the People's Party favored an early convention and the running of their own ticket on their own platform, but when the managers decided otherwise and it became evident that the program included an alliance with the Democrats the party, with substantial unanimity, went to work in good faith to make the best fight they could. They expected, as they had a right to do, that Democrats would play fair, and that Populists would not anywhere be expected to yield more than had been granted by the national convention.

It was presumed that in all the States the Populists would vote their own party ticket, with Bryan and Watson at the head, followed by Populist Electors. That course would have insured the entire Populist vote for Bryan and Watson, and the full strength of the party vote would have been disclosed when the vote for Watson Electors was counted. As it turned out, however, in some of the States, as in Kansas and North Dakota, for example, it was arranged that Democratic Electors should go on the Populist ticket in consideration of Democratic support of the Populist State ticket. This was a deliberate betrayal of Watson by men who, from every honorable consideration, ought to have stood by him to the end.

This is true especially of Kansas. At a time and under circumstances that tested the mettle of the man and disclosed the purity of his motives and the high estimate he placed on an honest and faithful compliance with pledges made to his fellow-men, Mr. Watson parted company with his Southern Democratic associates in Congress and joined hands with Kansas Populists and with the independents of the Northwest. Livingston and Winn and Moses, elected as Alliance men, preferred to be classed with Democrats and to work with their party, while Watson, elected as a Democrat, but pledged to do whatever he could to work Alliance principles into law, preferred to identify himself with men pledged like himself, rather than to cooperate with a party that had nothing in common with the Alliance.

More than this, Watson's acceptance of the second place on the ticket was much against his judgment and desire. He at first refused to consider the proposition to place him in that position. Nothing but the most earnest and urgent appeals of his friends moved him to change his mind. He was opposed on principle to the whole fusion business, and he felt that to become a party to it, and especially to be placed at its head, was to sacrifice his party, his friends, and himself.

In view of these facts he was in honor entitled to the support of every Kansas Populist. But instead, the managers in that State traded him off for Democratic votes for their State ticket. The understanding was that in case the national Democratic ticket was successful, the Kansas portion of the national administration's patronage should be disposed of wholly in the interest of that party.

By way of showing how deep as well as how filthy the corruption of "practical politics" among reformers had become at that time, it may be added that when the failure of the national Democracy and the success of Kansas Demo-Populism became recognized facts, instead of "taking their medicine" as they had prepared it, they demanded to share in the patronage of the Populist State administration in Kansas. Had it stopped at the demand, the full measure of the transaction would not have been exposed to the public. But the new Populist Governor, John W. Leedy,[1] proceeded to distribute his favors among the hungry in each of the grand divisions of the "triple alliance"—Democrat, Silver Republican, and Populist.

Had the distribution of offices been conducted according to the vote cast by the then different parties, it would have borne the semblance of a disposition to dole out a gratuity along lines of fairness. But it was not done that way. The vote for Leedy was 168,041, of which Democrats did not, probably, cast more than 45,000 (as the Democratic vote for Governor in Kansas in 1894, when a full State ticket was run, with David Overmeyer,[2] a popular and able Democrat, at the head, was 26,709, when Lewelling, the Populist candidate for Governor, received 118,329). But although they were enti-

1. John W. Leedy, a farmer near LeRoy, Kansas, had been a Democrat until joining the People's party in 1892. In that year he was elected as a Populist to the state senate, where he proved a less than enthusiastic supporter of Populist principles. Elected governor in 1896, after being endorsed by the Democrats following his Populist nomination, Leedy had a rather unsatisfactory administration and was defeated when he sought reelection in 1898. In 1901 he left Kansas for Canada.

2. David Overmeyer, a Topeka attorney, was a traditional conservative Democrat in nearly all particulars, opposing woman suffrage, prohibition, Republican "paternalism," and Populist radicalism while exalting the Democratic commitment to "individual liberty" and limited government. As a Kansas delegate to the Democratic National Convention in 1892, he had seconded Cleveland's nomination.

tled to no consideration at the hands of the State administration, the Governor treated them as if they were entitled to at least one-third, and this required the ignoring of many faithful, competent, and deserving Populists.

Returning to the Presidential elections, there were divisions made in some of the States, so that both Democrat and Populist Electors were placed on each of the party tickets. This was done in the following named States, and the division was as here stated:

States.	Democratic Electors	Populist Electors
Arkansas	5	3
California	5	4
Colorado	2	1
Connecticut	5	1
Idaho	2	1
Illinois	20	4
Indiana	10	5
Iowa	10	3
Kentucky	11	2
Louisiana	4	4
Massachusetts	13	2
Michigan	9	4
Minnesota	4	5
Missouri	13	4
Montana	1	2
Nebraska	4	4
New Jersey	9	1
North Carolina	5	6
Ohio	18	5
Oregon	2	2
Pennsylvania	28	4
Utah	1	2

Washington	1	2
West Virginia	4	2
Wisconsin	9	3
Wyoming	2	1

NOTE: Oregon had one Silver Republican Elector on the Democratic ticket.

When the electoral votes were counted it appeared that Mr. Watson had received part of the vote in ten of the States, Mr. Sewall receiving the others as follows.

	Sewall.	Watson.
Arkansas	5	3
Louisiana	4	4
Missouri	13	4
Montana	2	1
Nebraska	4	4
North Carolina	6	5
South Dakota	2	2
Utah	2	1
Washington	2	2
Wyoming	2	1
Totals	42	27

The total vote received by Mr. Sewall was 149, which is a little more than five votes to Mr. Watson's one, when, according to the returns of the elections of 1894, the Populists must have had in 1896 nearly one-third the total vote of Mr. Bryan. Watson ought to have received one-third instead of one-fifth of the Bryan Electors, and if he had been treated fairly he would have received that proportion.

The management of Populist party affairs during all of the two years, 1895–'96, up to the time of holding the national convention, the manner of conducting the convention, and the management of the campaign after the convention and on the day of election, alienated at least one-third of the membership of the People's Party. The largest defection was in the Southern States, where a movement was inaugurated looking to a calling together of the National Committee for a general conference.

By way of determining the extent of the feeling in this direction, and also to collect materials on which further action, if any were deemed proper, might be based, Mr. George F. Washburn of Massachusetts, a member of the National Committee, addressed a letter to a large number of representative Populists, asking their views in relation to the proposed conference.[3] This letter was given to the press on January 11, 1897.

A large number of answers to this letter was received within the next ten or twelve days, and they were published in the *Boston Herald* on January 25, 1897. Here are sample extracts from some of those letters—enough to show the tenor of all:

> Senator Allen—The Populist party must march under its own banner. It must not be absorbed by any other party, and while I fully approve of the action taken by the party last fall, respecting the nomination of Mr. Bryan, and cooperating with the Democrats and Republicans who believed in monetary reform, there was never a moment when it was my desire or wish that the party should be absorbed by another, or be disintegrated.

3. George F. Washburn of Boston had directed (and personally financed) the Chicago headquarters of the Populist National Executive Committee during the 1896 campaign. A moderate mid-roader, he had only reluctantly accepted the Populist nomination of Bryan. His 1897 "Appeal to the Populists of the United States" was more a manifesto than a letter of inquiry as suggested by Peffer. In it, he urged Populists to break away from the less radical Democratic party in order to preserve their own party's integrity, discounted the importance of silver compared to the issues of paper money and government ownership, and proposed a Populist national conference to determine the party's course. See *Boston Herald*, January 11, 1897.

Senator Butler, Chairman of the National Committee—I agree with you that we should push other issues to the front along with the free coinage of silver, and demand not only the abolition of the national banks, but that the amount of full legal tender money shall be increased to meet the needs of population and business. And on account of the conduct of the railroads in the last campaign, it seems to me that the time is ripe to push our transportation plank along boldly, side by side with the financial plank.

Senator Peffer—The Democrats at Chicago made a bold advance, and in their new declaration inserted one of the Populist doctrines—that relating to silver coinage. But that is a very small beginning, and I see no evidence of a disposition to move one step beyond it. That does not satisfy the true Populist. I have no sympathy with the Democratic party. I left its ranks forty-five years ago and do not expect to return. There is nothing left for us, as Populists, to do but to hold up our banner and stand by it, come weal or come woe. Principle before policy.

Colonel S. F. Norton, Illinois, member of National Committee, and voted against Mr. Bryan in the Populist national convention as a candidate for the head of the ticket—Yes, we can consistently stand for the preservation of the greenback currency, leaving Democrats and Republicans to kick shins and pull hair over the twin relics of barbarism [i.e., gold and silver]. I see [John] Sherman is out in a letter in favor of maintaining the present volume of greenbacks. Perhaps even he will yet want to join the "Pops." I am not a Democrat, nor am I a Republican. There is no course for Populists in the future except straight ahead under the banner of greenbackism. I am satisfied that the vast majority of our party desire to push the fight along the line of paper money against coin money.

J. H. ("Cyclone") Davis,[4] Texas, member of National Committee—I indorse the sentiment and tone of your letter fully. It came, too, in exact time. I would like to see all reform forces united along the lines you suggest.

M. C. Rankin,[5] Indiana, member of National Committee and Treasurer of the People's Party—Your appeal is all right. We stand for scientific money. I think the appeal excellent and well timed. By standing firm we can force the Democrats to advance to our position. Our main issue must be full legal tender paper money issued and controlled by the government alone. I favor a conference in February at some central point.

General Paul Van Dervoort, Nebraska, President National Reform Press Association—I strongly favor a national conference. There is a general demand for a national conference at once. My mail is filled with letters urging that one be held in Memphis next month. Don't wait to correspond with the leaders about this, but issue your call at once, and it will meet with general approval. You have raised the issue and called for independent party action

---

4. James H. Davis of Sulphur Springs, Texas, was a lawyer, editor of the *Alliance Vindicator*, and one of the most popular Populist orators. For a description of Davis and his speaking style, and an explanation of the origin of his nickname, see Roscoe C. Martin, *The People's Party in Texas: A Study in Third Party Politics* (Austin: University of Texas Bulletin, 1933), 120–123. Davis helped organize the People's party and was a member of the party's national committee from 1892 to 1900, by which time he was a leader of the Texas fusionists. In 1914 he was elected as a Democrat to Congress.

5. Morton C. Rankin, a lumber dealer of Terre Haute, Indiana, had been an active Greenbacker in the 1870s and 1880s. In 1890 he helped organize the Indiana People's party, and in 1891 the Cincinnati Conference, which launched the national party, elected him treasurer of the Populist National Executive Committee, a position he thereafter retained. He was an unsuccessful Populist nominee for Congress in both 1894 and 1896.

and you must now lead off in the next step for a national conference.

James R. Sovereign, member of National Committee and Master Workman of the Knights of Labor—I most heartily agree with the principal points in your letter. I will certainly oppose all political parties that have not the honesty and the courage to take a firm stand against the retirement of the greenbacks.

W. Morris Deisher, President of the Central Bimetallic League of Pennsylvania—I am right in line with your views. I want the nationalization of all public utilities just as fast as we can get them, but the three factors you name are vital and we must secure them or forfeit the right of American independence.

S. S. Harvey, member of National Committee and Mayor of Pensacola, Florida—It affords me pleasure to feel that I can still fully agree with you as I have in the past and now fully do on the lines laid down in your circular. . . .

Wharton Barker,[6] editor of the *American*, Philadelphia—If the People's party can be kept on the platform you make for it in your open letter, you need not fear the result of the elections in 1898 and 1900.

James H. Ferris, Illinois, member of National Committee— Your appeal is timely. The Populists are not Democrats and must not be dealt with as such.

C. Vincent, member of National Committee and editor of the *Nonconformist*, Indianapolis, Ind.—I sympathize with you in your statement of the situation. Like yourself, I much regretted the turn things took at St. Louis, but after the convention, throughout the campaign, I loyally sup-

6. In 1898, hoping to head off another fusion campaign in 1900, disgruntled middle-of-the-road Populists met in Cincinnati and nominated Wharton Barker for the presidency, at least partially because of a belief that he could finance the campaign himself.

ported its action. I was glad, indeed, to have such a communication as yours to present to the people, and the
source from which it came will be of great assistance in securing a respectful hearing from our party. . . .

J. E. Leslie, member of National Committee and Chairman
[of the] People's Party Committee of Pennsylvania—Permit me to compliment you upon a paper at once timely
and to the point. It has the right ring and will do much to
encourage our disheartened, disgusted, and disgruntled
brothers. The idea of a conference is a good one.

There were many more, but these cover the whole ground, and
while a majority are silent on the question of calling a conference,
there is apparent unanimity on the matter of maintaining the integrity of the party; that is, keeping up the party organization.

Mr. Washburn did not feel authorized to call a conference, as that
could be regularly done only by the National Committee of the
party through its chairman. But at the next meeting of the National
Reform Press Association at Memphis, Tennessee, on February 22,
1897, a resolution was adopted favoring such a conference and appointing a committee to look after the matter. This committee addressed a communication to [Populist National] Chairman Butler
(Senator Butler of North Carolina, temporary chairman of the St.
Louis nominating convention) requesting him to get the committee
together for the purposes stated in the Memphis resolution of the
press people. Chairman Butler, instead of calling the committee together, addressed a letter to each member asking him whether he
thought such a meeting ought to be called, and with his letter to each
committeeman Chairman Butler enclosed his own opinion, written
out at length, opposing the conference and arguing against it.

As might have been expected, and as Chairman Butler intended,
a majority of the committee did not see any good to come from
such a conference, and it was not called.

XI
Results of Fusion Movement

Although the effort to get Chairman Butler to call together the National Committee for a general conference failed, through the insistence of the committee appointed by the National Reform Press Association at Memphis in February, 1897, a meeting for conference purposes was arranged for June 15 at Omaha. The following Associated Press dispatch shows how it ended:

Omaha, Nebraska, June 15.—Diplomatic relations between the middle-of-the-road Populists and the Liberals are strained. The middle-of-the-road crowd, under the leadership of Milton Park[1] of Texas, is entrenched at the Thurston Rifles Armory, and the liberal wing, with Senator Marion Butler in command, has a strong position at the Millard Hotel. Conciliatory notes from the Butler wing have been sent to the Park wing, but the latter has so far shown no sign of yielding any part of its program. This, Mr. Park announced, is undying opposition to fusion, the refusal to recognize Mr. Bryan until he renounces his Democracy, and a convention in July, 1898, to nominate a national ticket for the campaign of 1900. Park

1. Milton Park was the editor of the *Southern Mercury* of Dallas, Texas, and a consistent opponent of fusion. In 1895 he was elected president of the National Reform Press Association.

is supported by the members of the Reform Press Association, which has just concluded its session here. He declared he will never surrender.

An agreement was reported to have been reached shortly before the adjournment of the conference, to the effect that the differences between the opposing factions should be submitted to the next regular convention of the party. The regularity of the proceeding by which this agreement was reached is in dispute.

The committee appointed by the Reform Press Association then called a conference of delegates, chosen in the usual way, to meet at Nashville, Tennessee, on July 4, 1897, at which place and time 355 accredited delegates were present from the States following:

Alabama	38	Missouri	17
Arkansas	15	Nebraska	2
Florida	4	Montana	3
Georgia	39	New Hampshire	1
Illinois	24	North Carolina	2
Indiana	12	Ohio	21
Iowa	7	Rhode Island	1
Kansas	2	Tennessee	13
Kentucky	9	Texas	80
Louisiana	13	Washington	1
Michigan	12	West Virginia	2
Minnesota	19	Wisconsin	1
Mississippi	7		

This conference, after a stormy session, resolved that a reorganization of the party on a straight Populist, anti-fusion basis was imperatively necessary to prevent the utter demoralizing of Populist voters and the ultimate absorption of many of them by the Democracy, and a committee, to be known as the Reorganization Committee, was appointed to carry out the plan outlined by the delegates in conference assembled. Milton Park of Texas, editor of the *Southern*

Mercury, at Dallas, was made chairman of the committee. The Re-organization Committee was authorized to call a national [party] convention whenever in its judgment such a proceeding ought to be had; or, if the committee should think it better, it was authorized to submit the matter to a referendum vote of the party membership.[2]

The committee called a convention which was held at Cincinnati on September 5, 1898, and during a two-day session it adopted a long address to the people and an anti-fusion platform, reaffirming Populist principles as set forth in the Omaha platform of 1892, with the addition of [the] referendum, and nominated a national ticket for 1900—Wharton Barker of Pennsylvania for President, Ignatius Donnelly[3] of Minnesota for Vice President—subject to the approval of the voters of the party by referendum.

After adopting the platform the report of the committee on plan of organization was read, and although adopted was again laid before the convention for the purpose of affording an opportunity to Mr. [James E.] McBride, a delegate from Michigan, to offer a resolution, the purpose of which was to submit the proposed plan of organization to the National Committee of the People's Party—the

2. Peffer initially argued against holding this Nashville conference because only the national committee was authorized to call a party conference and because only mid-roaders could be expected to attend, making it unrepresentative of the party. But his increasing estrangement from Butler and Weaver and his growing conviction that their policies were leading to the absorption of the Populists into the Democratic party led him to endorse the conference when it met. The delegates, he wrote, did not seek to injure the party by attacking Butler "but to save the party by getting control, at the proper time and in the proper way, of the party machinery." See Topeka *Advocate*, April 28, July 14, 1897.

3. Ignatius Donnelly was a flamboyant orator, editor, and author long active in third-party politics. A former Congressman as a Republican, he then became a Greenbacker, Granger, Alliance legislator, and Populist. He was the author of the famous preamble to the Omaha Platform of the People's party. For an excellent biography, see Martin Ridge, *Ignatius Donnelly: The Portrait of a Politician* (Chicago: University of Chicago Press, 1962).

committee appointed by the regular party convention at St. Louis in July, 1896—and to the Reorganization Committee acting jointly.

The resolution, after a brief debate, was tabled by a vote of 210 to 76, whereupon, after the defeat of several other motions on the part of the minority delegates, Mr. McBride and his adherents retired and adopted an address setting forth the reasons for their withdrawal, as follows:

To the People's Party of the United States:

On behalf of our delegates who attended the meeting called at Cincinnati by some of the old members of the People's party, we submit the following protest to the action of that body:

We attended the convention for the purpose of preserving harmony among those who espoused the straight, pure and simple People's party doctrine. But those who controlled the convention were prompted by some purpose, provoking them to override every effort made to promote the interests of the party. The convention proceeded properly to establish a referendum system through which nominees of the party for the several offices could be selected by the members of the party voting in their respective precincts. When we sought to have the National Central and National Organization committees put the program into effect, within an hour they refused, disregarding the plan adopted by themselves, and immediately proceeded to the nomination of President and Vice President; and by their action we believe they have placed themselves outside the regular organization of the People's party, and created for themselves a new party. Thereupon quite one-half of the delegates withdrew, preferring to remain loyal to the People's party and willing to trust to future developments to remedy party difficulties.

We implore the Populists of every State to pay no heed to nor to attach importance to this small sloughing off of party timber, but to maintain an aggressive warfare on the line hith-

erto followed, to build up and preserve our State and local organizations, in accordance with the recommendations of the
National Organization Committee, as adopted at Nashville,
on July 4, 1897, and the subsequent agreement between our
two national committees at Omaha, on June 15, 1898, relying
on the patriotism and good judgment of men advocating both
policies of party management to heal their differences before
the time fixed for our regular national convention.

The delegates joining in this address were from the States of
Arkansas, Illinois, Indiana, Kentucky, Michigan, Missouri, Ohio,
and Tennessee.

There was some irregularity about the call for this convention,
and that accounts for the hard work of the Committee on Creden-
tials. Some of the delegates had no official authority to show for
their presence. Neither a list of delegates nor their number was
published. There were no delegates from the Eastern States.

The returns of the elections in Southern States for 1895, '96,
and '98 show the effect of the fusion movement on the Populist
vote in that region. In Alabama, in 1892, the Populist vote for President was 85,181 and the Republican vote was 9,197. In 1896 the
Republican vote for President was 54,737, and no Populist vote is
recorded, showing that the Populists—those of them that voted—
favored the Republican ticket, for the Democratic vote that year
was nearly 8,000 votes short of its record four years before. For
1898 in that State there is no Populist vote recorded on Governor,
but the Republican gain was considerable.

In Georgia the Populist vote on President in 1892 was 42,937,
and that of the Republicans was 48,306. In 1894 the Republican
vote on Governor was 96,888, and no Populist vote is returned for
that year. In 1896 the Populist vote on Governor was 85,832, and
no Republican vote. The vote of these two parties on President that
year was [Republican] 60,091; Populist, none. For Governor in

1898 no Populist vote is returned, though 51,580 Republican votes were cast.

In Texas Populists cast 99,688 votes for President in 1892, and 149,857 votes two years later for Controller. In 1895 their vote was increased to 159,224 on Governor. In 1896, for President, the Bryan fusion ticket received 370,434 votes; the Republican ticket received 167,520 votes, which was more than twice that party's vote in 1892. If we subtract the Democratic vote of 1895, which was 241,882, from the combined vote of the fusion-Democratic-Populists in 1896, we have 128,552 as approximately the number of Populists that voted with the Democrats that year, and this is a falling off of the Populist vote of the year before equal to 30,067. The Republican vote of 1896 was 86,076 ahead of its vote in 1892, which was the largest in the record of Texas Republicans before 1896.

These returns from three States casting the largest Populist vote in the South show that the loss has been enormous on the part of the People's party, and that while in Alabama and Georgia Republicans are gaining most of the Populist loss, in Texas the Democrats are getting most of the retiring Populist vote.

In Ohio, Populists polled 52,675 votes for Governor in 1895. They have not had a ticket since. The Democrat gain in [the] Presidential vote of 1896 over that of 1892 was 73,379, while [the] Republican gain on [the] same votes was 120,804, indicating that most of the Populist vote in 1896 went to the Republicans.

In Iowa, in 1897, the regular Populist State convention indorsed the Democrat State ticket and resolved to vote with the Democrats. Straight Populists rebelled, held a State convention, put out a straight ticket, which received 4,268 votes. Two years before the Populist vote was 32,118.

Illinois Populists, in 1894, cast 59,793 votes; four years later they dropped to 7,893.

Indiana Populists, in 1894, polled a vote of 29,388. The figures were reduced to 6,016 four years later.

These are four representative Northern States—Ohio, Indiana, Illinois, and Iowa. In all of them the Populist vote is practically eliminated.

The following tables (pp. 168-169) will be helpful in studying the decline of Populism.[4] The tables show the vote of the leading parties in the State since 1890. The Prohibition and National [Gold] Democrat vote is not included, the object being to show the growth and decay of the Populist vote and how, probably, the change has affected or will affect the Democratic and Republican vote in future.

In Kansas and Nebraska the People's party got into the hands of machine politicians several years ago, and it is still there. In Nebraska, as in Kansas, Democrats have been trading off State patronage for that which is expected to come from the national administration in case of national success. In Kansas last year (1898) the Democratic State convention actually nominated as their own ticket the whole of the Populist State officers then on duty, and this before the Populist State convention, then in session, had reached the nominating part of the program, and when it was reached the whole ticket was nominated at one time in one vote, and that by acclamation. It was their own ticket, but nominated first by the Democratic convention.

This familiar spontaneousness on the part of the Democrats is

4. This reliance on statistical data—whether voting returns, census reports, or banking records—is an obvious characteristic of Peffer's style. One historian has concluded that even Peffer's speeches were "distinguished mainly by their plethora of statistics" (Roger A. Fischer, "Rustic Rasputin: William A. Peffer in Color Cartoon Art, 1891-1899," *Kansas History* 11 [Winter 1988-1989]: 222). Peffer's contemporaries, of course, were similarly impressed. William Allen White, in fact, once described Peffer as not primarily a political leader but "essentially a statistician." If given a number, White wrote, Peffer would promptly begin "figuring out how many times the square root of the number will go into the currency per capita providing the endless chain in the Treasury is hung over the moon and worked with compressed air drawing a quadrillion gallons of water a minute. Peffer will be happy only in the rapt contemplation of things ecstatic like logarythms [sic] and parabolas and catachylams and other things in three syllables." *Emporia Gazette*, May 23, 1899.

TABLE XI-1

Year	Office	Democratic Votes	Republican Votes	Populist Votes	Republican and Populist	Democratic and Populist
ALABAMA						
1890	Governor	139,910	42,440	....	....	....
1892	Governor	126,959	....	115,522	....	....
1892	President	138,138	9,197	85,181	....	....
1894	Governor	110,865	....	83,283	....	....
1896	Governor	128,541	....	....	89,290	....
1896	President	130,307	54,737	....	....	....
1898	Governor	111,936	22,162	....	....	....
GEORGIA						
1890	Governor	105,365	....	....	....	....
1892	President	129,361	48,306	42,937	....	....
1894	Governor	121,049	96,888	....	....	....
1896	Governor	120,827	....	85,832	....	....
1896	President	94,232	60,091	....	....	....
1898	Governor	118,557	51,580	....	....	....
TEXAS						
1890	Governor	262,432	77,742	....	....	....
1892	President	239,148	88,444	99,688	....	....
1894	Controller	216,240	62,575	149,857	....	....
1895	Governor	241,882	55,405	159,224	....	....
1896	President	....	167,520	....	....	370,434
1898	Governor	285,074	....	132,348	....	....
OHIO						
1891	Governor	365,228	386,739	23,472	....	....
1892	President	404,115	405,187	14,850	....	....
1893	Governor	352,347	433,342	15,583	....	....
1895	Governor	334,519	427,141	52,675	....	....
1896	President	477,494	525,991	....	....	....
1897	Governor	401,750	429,915	....	....	....
ILLINOIS						
1892	President	426,281	399,288	22,207	....	....
1894	Treasurer	322,459	445,886	59,793	....	....
1896	Governor	....	587,587	....	....	474,270
1896	President	....	607,130	....	....	464,632
1898	Treasurer	405,490	448,940	7,893	....	....

INDIANA

Year	Office				
1890	Secy/State	233,881	214,302	17,354	....
1892	President	262,740	255,216	22,208	....
1894	Secy/State	238,732	283,405	29,388	....
1896	President	305,573	323,754	....	....
1898	Secy/State	265,896	282,795	6,016	....

IOWA

Year	Office				
1892	President	196,367	219,795	20,595	....
1894	Secy/State	149,980	229,376	34,907	....
1896	President	223,741	289,293	....	....
1897	Governor	194,514	224,501	4,268	....
1898	Secy/State	173,000	236,524	3,372	....

KANSAS

Year	Office				
1890	Governor	71,357	115,025	108,972	....
1892	President	....	157,237	163,111	....
1894	Governor	26,709	148,697	118,320	....
1896	President	....	159,641	....	171,810
1898	Governor	....	149,853	....	133,963

NEBRASKA

Year	Office				
1892	President	24,943	87,213	83,134	....
1894	Governor	....	94,613	....	97,815
1896	President	....	102,304	....	115,880
1898	Governor	....	92,982	....	95,703

easily accounted for when we read in an interview of John W. Breidenthal, State Bank Commissioner of Kansas, and conceded to be the best informed man in the State on Demo-Populism, with W. E. Curtis, a Chicago newspaper correspondent, that the Northwest is for Bryan in 1900.

This friendly mixing of parties from year to year brings the membership into an alliance which confuses doctrine. A man cannot long be on two sides of any question and retain a clear view of his own convictions.

As the fusion business began in the Seventh Congressional District of Kansas and has been nurtured there continuously ever since, it was natural that the idea of a permanent union between Democrats and Populists should suggest a name for the hybrid, and the

Congressman who was first elected by a fusion vote invented the new name. On page 35 of the second edition of the *Congressional Directory* for the Fifty-fifth Congress is recorded the fact that Jerry Simpson, originally a Populist, was elected to the Fifty-fifth Congress as a Demo-Populist.

A further effect of the fusion of 1896 is the evident expectation of the leaders of the Democratic party that Populists will remain in the service begun in '96, and the managers of the Populist party are prepared to make the alliance perpetual. Chairman Butler of the Populist National Committee dropped into a seat beside the writer of this one day in the Senate, stating that Mr. W. J. Bryan desired to deposit some money with him to be used in advancing the silver cause, and he (Butler) asked the writer's advice as to what he ought to do about receiving the money. The advice was quickly given: "Don't take it." And he didn't.[5] The money, $1,500, was placed in the hands of Senator Allen of Nebraska, who, sometime afterwards in a personal statement in the Senate, said he had secured the investment of the money in interest bearing securities, which were deposited with R. B. Nixon, financial clerk of the Senate, for safe keeping. The money was to be used, Senator Allen stated, in furthering the cause of bimetallism.

And it is understood among Populists of Democratic leanings that Messrs. Allen and Butler are both Bryan men, and that they advise and will advise the same sort of a union with the Democracy in 1900 that was effected in 1896. Indeed, so far as Mr. Butler is concerned, he openly advocates what he calls cooperation with any other party or faction whenever votes can be given or gained by either party for silver in connection with a division of offices. His

5. For Butler's own explanation of his decision not to accept Bryan's money, which derived from the royalties from the Democrat's book on the 1896 campaign, *The First Battle*, see Robert F. Durden, *The Climax of Populism: The Election of 1896* (Lexington: University of Kentucky Press, 1965), 160n. Durden's volume provides a brief account, from the perspective of Butler, of the conflict within Populist ranks after 1896, which saw Butler and Peffer often take opposing positions.

strongest argument, from his standpoint, in favor of retaining the Populist organization is that it can be used advantageously for trading purposes.

This policy has been frequently questioned, and Mr. Butler, as Chairman of the National Committee, has often been asked for advice. Early in 1898, when an election was in prospect in Oregon, John C. Young, chairman of the Oregon Populist State Central Committee, criticized a letter of Chairman Butler, which he, Young, construed to advise fusion of Populists with Democrats in Oregon; and, under date of Washington, D.C., February 14, 1898, Chairman Butler replied to Chairman Young, saying among many other things: "I am not in favor of fusion with any party, and I am not even in favor of cooperation unless such cooperation can be on fair and honorable terms and the result of which will be an advancement of our principles and, therefore, a victory for the people." And again, when referring to Young's doubts about the sincerity of Democrats, Mr. Butler says: "By all means test their sincerity before the next campaign opens. In short, make them a fair proposition for an honorable cooperation, not based on office alone, but covering the great undying principles in the fight."

This letter, in full, was printed in the *Caucasian*, Mr. Butler's paper, of Raleigh, N.C., in the latter part of March, 1898. The National Chairman's argument is that Populists should cooperate on "fair and honorable terms" with any and all parties that favor the silver movement and show their sincerity by dividing the offices.

XII
The Difference between Democracy and Populism

To understand the creed of the Populists it is necessary first to reflect a moment on their view of social, financial, and political conditions at the time this new party movement began in 1890.

Quoting from a speech delivered by the writer hereof before a convention of straight Populists at Des Moines, Iowa, on August 19, 1897:

> Our government, from the beginning, had been under control of one or the other of two great parties, dividing on questions relating to the constitutional powers of the State and national governments. They differed about tariffs, internal improvements, banks, and the extension of slavery into the Territories. But with the great war new forces came into play. Our enormous debt was better than a gold mine to the speculator. The usurer preyed on the people's substance. Our public lands were squandered and a stupendous railway system was developed. Our currency was funded in coin bonds; the coinage of silver dollars was discontinued; the word "coin" was construed to mean gold, and the New York banks took charge of the country's finances. Misfortunes befell the people. The general level of prices fell to the cost line and below it; invention multiplied men with muscles of iron and nerves of steel, and immigration swelled the ranks of the unemployed. Debt

had overtaken us. Nine million homes had been mortgaged, and in our great cities an average of 77 in every 100 families were paying for the privilege of living there. In the country at large 52 per cent of the people were living in rented property, and in New York City the proportion was 94 per cent. Agriculture was prostrate and labor was manacled. The earth had come under the domination of landlords; forests and coal mines were owned by syndicates; railway companies were in combination; wealth and political influence had been usurped by a few men, and the seat of government was transferred to New York.

These conditions forced new problems forward, and the political parties then existing were not competent to solve them. They had not been formed for such a purpose. . . . That government by the people might not perish from the earth, a new alignment of voters had become necessary, and the People's Party was formed. It proclaimed a new doctrine; it published a new creed. It grounded itself on the equality of human rights. It declared that the earth is the heritage of the people, and that wealth belongs to him who creates it; that the means for the distribution of the products of labor ought to belong to the people and be operated by their agents; that money should be provided by the government and distributed through public agencies, and that borrowers might procure its use at an annual charge not exceeding 2 per cent, which is equal to two-thirds of the net average savings of the whole people.

These four great ideas—land, labor, transportation, and money—cover the whole field of human exertion, and they include all the reforms needed at the time except one, and this the new party provided for in its submitting the proposition that the people reserve to themselves, in their capacity as individual citizens, the right to propose legislation, and to vote on every great measure of public policy before it shall take effect as law.

In addition to these, and as matter of detail, this new party favors the popular election of the President, the Vice President, United States Senators; it favors postal savings banks, a graduated income tax, and the abolition of landlordism; and it favors the free and unlimited coinage of silver and gold at the present legal ratio.

The People's Party was based on the fact that the other parties had not taken up any of these questions which Populists regarded as of primary importance, and the correct disposition of which was necessary to the permanent welfare of the people.

It is to be observed that these questions were not only new, but they belonged to a new class of ideas; that is to say, a class of ideas not before brought into politics; and of all parties, large or small, ever flitting over the public stage, the Democratic party was and is least able to handle them. That party is based on an idea that belonged to the last century, an idea developed in discussions that arose among members of our first President's Cabinet, with respect to the power properly attaching to federal authority. The party was born in and for other times. It was consecrated to an issue which was finally determined against it in war by the sword. While claiming for itself the virtues of conservatism, it is now, as it has always been, the only revolutionary party in the country big enough to be capable of doing much harm.

Fortunately for us at this time we have outgrown the heresies of the strict constructionists. Ever since the beginning of our great war for the preservation of the union our government has been conducted on the theory of its founders—that the people of the United States constitute a nation—but the Democratic party has not yet come to comprehend it. Under the influence of this national sentiment, we have reached the front rank of nations, and new opportunities are now before us for greater and grander achievements—opportunities which Democratic doctrines and policies would let pass unimproved to the nation's shame, rather than let some pet party theory be nullified.

There is positively nothing in common between the principles of Democracy and Populism. Their foundation ideas are different. Populists believe in the exercise of national authority in any and every case where the general welfare will be promoted thereby. The Democratic party is opposed to this.

[Transportation]

Populists believe that the people ought to own and, through their government, operate railroads and other national monopolies. The Democratic party is opposed to the government making any sort of internal improvements except what may be necessary for military purposes.

Early in the century, Congress appropriated money to open and improve national roads leading out from the capital in different directions. The first appropriation for this purpose was made in 1806. The first road begun, and the only one ever completed to any considerable length, was known as the Cumberland road, passing over portions of Maryland, Virginia, and Pennsylvania, into Ohio, and on west to St. Louis. The last appropriation by Congress for this road was in 1838.

A question arose relative to the constitutional authority of Congress to build roads in the States. Democrats opposed it. As to States north of the Ohio River and west of Pennsylvania, the subject was provided for in the acts organizing Territorial governments there and in the acts admitting the States formed out of the Northwest Territory. But as to Maryland, Virginia, and Pennsylvania, they were of the original thirteen and they, according to Democratic State's rights doctrine, could not tolerate the erection of toll gates and the collection of tolls by the general government on roads running across any part of their territory. The subject was deemed of sufficient importance to be discussed by Presidents in messages to Congress, and that body frequently debated it. An adjustment finally was reached by Congress authorizing the cession of the road

to the States named on condition that they would keep them open
and in good repair. Acts accepting the possession were passed by
the Legislatures of the States named and duly approved by the Gov-
ernors thereof, and thus was a great constitutional question disposed [of] without settling anything. But in 1840 the Democratic
party, when it held its first national convention, after first declaring
"that the federal government is one of limited powers," resolved,
second, "That the constitution does not confer on the general government the power to commence and carry on a general system of
internal improvements."

That is the doctrine of the Democratic party today.

The Populist would not think of stopping at the line of a Democratic State if he were building a government railway.

[Finance]

If there is any part of the Populist's creed which he regards as
more important than another, and which, therefore, may be taken as
leading, it is that which demands the issue and circulation of national money—money made solely for use as a money, made by authority of the people for their use, money that they will at any and all
times be responsible for, money that persons in business can procure
on good security at cost, money handled only by public agencies,
thus doing away with all bank issues of paper to be used as money.

The Omaha platform is taken by all Populists to be the foundation of their party beliefs. The principles there enunciated are to
them what the Apostles' creed is to Christians—a compendium of
their faith. It was adopted by the party's first national convention,
which met at Omaha, Nebraska, on July 4, 1892, and is, therefore,
the party's first official utterance. Here is an exact copy of its financial plank:

We demand a national currency, safe, sound, and flexible,
issued by the general government only, a full legal tender for

all debts, public and private, and that without the use of banking corporations, a just and efficient means of distribution direct to the people, at a tax not exceeding 2 per cent per annum, to be provided as set forth in the subtreasury plan of the Farmers' Alliance or some better system; also by payments in discharge of its obligations for public improvements.

In order that the underlying idea of the Populists' monetary scheme may be clearly understood, it is necessary that the "subtreasury plan of the Farmers' Alliance" be kept in mind. That "plan" originated among the cotton planters of the Southern States. Dr. Macune, mentioned in the first of these articles, is credited with its paternity. The cotton planters had long been in the habit of transacting their business through local merchants, warehousemen, and bankers. They purchased farm supplies—groceries, clothing, etc., from the merchants on time—until their crops could be turned into money; they stored their cotton in warehouses until they were ready to sell, and in the meantime borrowed currency from the banks to meet time obligations at maturity, using warehouse receipts as collateral.

After the great war, with the country in many places devastated, warehouses destroyed, State bank currency taxed out of existence, transportation facilities greatly impaired, and the labor system all out of joint, the planters found it exceedingly difficult to start again and get ahead. They had to pay about 100 per cent above cost and carriage for the merchandise they had to procure; the warehouse people charged them exorbitant prices for storage; and bankers demanded from 1 to 2 per cent a month for loans.

To secure relief from these three sources of oppression, Dr. Macune and his associates proposed that public warehouses be built, wherein cotton might be stored at reasonable charges, the certificates of deposit, during their life, to be used in the community as currency at 80 per cent of the value of the cotton in store, and to be canceled and destroyed when surrendered on removal of the property. It was a scheme to utilize the value of their produce to help themselves without being robbed on the way to market.

During the excitement occasioned by the debates in Congress and in the press on the silver coinage question Mr. Secretary Windom[1] proposed a plan for utilizing silver as money without coining it. A brief statement of the Windom idea is printed at page 74 of the Finance Report of the Secretary of the Treasury for the year 1889. It is as follows:

> Issue Treasury notes against deposits of silver bullion at the market price of silver when deposited, payable on demand in such quantities of silver bullion as will equal in value, at the date of presentation, the number of dollars expressed on the face of the notes of the market price of silver, or in gold, at the option of the government; or in silver dollars at the option of the holder. Repeal the compulsory feature of the present coinage act.

A bill drawn by the Treasury department of this plan was introduced in Congress and was known as the Windom bill. It was a simple, plain proposition, simply to issue Treasury notes (to be used as currency) against deposits of silver, and when the notes are surrendered deliver the silver or as much of it as will save the government from loss.

The "subtreasury plan of the Farmers' Alliance" was drawn on the lines of the Windom bill. It proposed to use cotton, corn,

1. William Windom of Minnesota was secretary of the Treasury under Republican President Benjamin Harrison from 1889 till his death in 1891. He had also been secretary of the Treasury under Republican President James Garfield in 1881 as well as a Representative and Senator from Minnesota. For a brief discussion of Windom and his silver plan, which did not gain the support of many Republicans, see Homer E. Socolofsky and Allan B. Spetter, *The Presidency of Benjamin Harrison* (Lawrence: University Press of Kansas, 1987), 25, 57–59.

wheat, oats, and tobacco just as Secretary Windom proposed to use silver—as a basis for a temporary circulating medium. Such a proceeding would require the erection of government warehouses in localities where the production of these staple products was large enough to warrant it. The subtreasury bill, as it was prepared by the farmers, fixed the value of such productions in a county at $500,000 for each of the last two preceding years before application for a warehouse or subtreasury should be considered, and the voters of a county were first to vote a donation of the site.

Section 2 of the bill provided:

> That the owner of cotton, wheat, corn, oats, or tobacco may deposit the same in the subtreasury nearest the point of its production, and receive therefor Treasury notes hereinafter provided for, equal at the date of deposit to 80 per cent of the net value of such products at the market price, said price to be determined by the Secretary of the Treasury, under rules and regulations by him prescribed, based upon the price current in the leading cotton, tobacco, or grain markets of the United States; but no deposit consisting in whole or part of cotton, tobacco, or grain imported into this country shall be received under the provisions of this act.

The other sections of the bill provide details for construction of the necessary buildings and conduct of the business as a part of the Treasury department's work. The warehouse receipts were to be transferable by indorsement. Property not redeemed within twelve months was to be sold. Within twelve months deposits were to be delivered to the holder of the receipt, on payment, in lawful money of the United States, of all charges for storage, insurance, etc.

Such was the "Subtreasury plan of the Farmers' Alliance," indorsed by that body in supreme national council at Ocala, Florida, December, 1890, and approved by the People's Party's first national convention at Omaha July 4, 1892. The bill was drawn with the Windom bill as a model. Farmers could see no good reason why their imperishable property was not as good security for a temporary currency as silver bullion, and such a currency at the time proposed would have been serviceable in some portions of the country, more especially in the Southern states. The bill was introduced in the House by Mr. Pickler of South Dakota[2] on February 17, 1890, and in the Senate by Mr. Vance of North Carolina, by request of the Farmers' Alliance and labor unions, on February 23, 1890. (The record dated one day later.)

The Democratic party would not entertain a proposition to indorse a scheme of that character, but it wanted the tax on State bank issues abolished that a local currency system may be reestablished in no respect as safe or as convenient as that proposed by the farmers.

That party is opposed to all kinds of legal tender paper money, as the Jones bill of January 23, 1895, showed plainly enough. The party platform of 1896—the Bryan platform—does not say a word in favor of that kind of money. What it does say is that all paper to be used as legal tender currency shall be issued by the government, and then it must be redeemed in coin. Here is the Bryan platform resolution on the subject:

> Congress alone has the power to coin and issue money, and President Jackson declared that this power could not be delegated to corporations or individuals. We, therefore, denounce the issuance of notes intended to circulate as money by national banks as in derogation of the constitution, and we demand that all paper which is made a legal tender for public and private debts, or which is receivable for duties to the United States, shall be issued by the government of the United States, and shall be redeemable in coin.

2. John A. Pickler was a Republican representative from South Dakota who served four terms in the House, 1889–1897. A lawyer and real estate developer, he was a vitriolic opponent of Populism despite his introduction of the subtreasury bill.

The Democratic party does not believe in national bank notes. These notes are not legal tender for any purpose, but the government takes them for everything except duties on imports, and they are secured by government bonds and by pledge of the nation to redeem every one of them. They pass current the same as coin and greenbacks, yet the Democratic party is opposed to them. Populists oppose them, not on constitutional grounds, as Democrats do, but on the ground that they are not as good money as pure legal tender government paper. Populists do not want private banks to have anything to do with issuing money. That, they claim, is an exercise of sovereign power, and they do not think that so great and important a power ought to be delegated to any private agency.

But the Democratic party opposes national bank notes on the ground that their issue is in "derogation of the constitution" and President Jackson. What that party desires in this direction is clearly set forth in this paragraph in its national platform of 1892—namely: "We recommend that the prohibitory 10 per çent tax on State bank issues be repealed." The 10 per cent tax is on State bank issues—that is, on the circulation of notes issued by State banks to circulate among the people in place of coin. That is the ideal currency of the modern as well as the ancient Democracy. And, as further showing the party's feeling toward the greenbacks, attention is called to the first and seventh sections of the Jones bill, already referred to. The first section provides for the issue and sale of $500,000,000 bonds to redeem the greenbacks and Treasury notes, and the seventh section provides that when the notes are redeemed they shall be "cancelled and destroyed."

And, as to silver coinage, the Democratic party, as a party, cares nothing about the ratio, as the Jones bill already referred to proves. That bill, prepared and urged as a party measure, commits the party to the theory of the gold monometallists, that silver should be valued by the gold standard, and that [bill], too, applied only to silver bullion brought to the mint by citizens of the United States. The Jones bill, as the reader will remember, proposed to coin only the market value of the bullion. If the quantity of bullion brought by a depositor was worth in the market—the gold price—say $100, just that amount of coin would be made out of it, though its coinage value might be $200. In other and, perhaps, plainer words, at the legal ratio of 16 to 1, the bullion would coin out $200, but at the bullion value, which is at the ratio of 32 to 1, it coins only $100, according to the provisions of the Jones bill. The bill is printed in full on page 2063, of volume 27, part 3, of the *Congressional Record*.

Briefly summing up on the money question, the Democratic party and the People's party are antipodal. They are wholly unlike. No compromise that would not smash the theories of both can possibly be made. The Populist believes in national legal tender paper money and favors no other kind, as an original proposition, and he does not believe interest charges ought to exceed 2 per cent a year, because labor does not produce more than 3 per cent above expense of production, and he thinks there ought to be a little profit on the use of money, left after the interest charge is paid. Democrats do not believe these propositions. They do not favor any kind of national paper money; and they insist on redeeming with coin all that we do have. The two parties cannot agree on these questions, and it is suicidal on the part of the Populists to try the experiment.

[Land]

The Populist idea of the land question finds no recognition in Democratic philosophy. Should the President of the United States, some time when coal miners are striking for better wages, recommend to Congress the passage of an act providing for the condemnation of the particular mining field for public use, to the end that the government might take possession of the mines, put the men at work at fair wages, and mine coal for the public, Democracy would join in a united chorus of denunciation of the Chief Executive, and we should have another series of lectures and essays on the usurpations of the President. Yet Populists think the President would be right in recommending such a measure and that Congress would be justified in enacting it.

And this again brings to view the essential difference between the two parties. It is fundamental. Populism teaches the doctrine that the rights and interests of the whole body of the people are superior and, therefore, paramount to those of individuals. The Populist believes in calling in the power of the people in every case where the public interests require it or will be promoted. He is opposed to private monopoly of any of the resources of nature; and he believes that wherever and whenever the public can be better, more justly, more economically served through public ownership and management of any line of business of a public character, that course ought to be adopted.

Democrats do not so believe. They denounce as usurpation every effort of government to serve the people itself, rather than to leave it to the avarice, cupidity, or inefficiency of private persons; whereas such a policy is in exact accord with the ideas of government entertained by men who swear by the Omaha platform and the "seven demands" of the Farmers' Alliance.

XIII
Résumé: Populism in Congress

When men of the new school first reached the national Congress they were curiously regarded. So much that was not true had been said and printed about them, and so little that was true was known about them away from home, that they were looked at, stared at, pointed out to strangers, and left alone to develop themselves. It was early discovered that they were orderly, modest, well-behaved men, unobtrusive, and not seeking notoriety. They were all cleanly and plainly attired, and not a profane man nor a drunkard among them. Watson and Otis were educated men. John Davis was well read and well informed—far above the average. The rest were fair, average men of their class.

This little band of Populists got together first at the rooms of Senator Peffer and held frequent conferences there; then they met at the residence of Mr. Watson. These conferences had a good effect in creating an agreeable union and strengthening their companionship; and during the two sessions of the Fifty-second Congress ('91–'93) the subjects discussed at the meetings related to ways and means for establishing Populism. The Populist movement was looked on by these men on the skirmish line as the beginning of a great and powerful organization, to be made up of dissatisfied voters in the two great parties, and destined to grow into power and wield a beneficent influence in the politics of the country.

With the death of the Fifty-second Congress several important changes took place in the Populist ranks. Two Kansas men—Clover and Otis, both radical men—retired, and Mr. Harris, a conservative man, came in as Congressman-at-large. He was indorsed and supported by the Democrats in State convention and at the polls. Two men—Bell and Pence, both specially interested in the silver question—came up from Colorado. In the Senate one addition to our number was made in the person of Senator Allen, who stood head and shoulders above all the rest in both Houses in point of physical and intellectual power. And Allen, when not goaded to extremes, was a conservative man.

The first session of the Fifty-third Congress was a called session, called for a purpose which brought the silver question to the front, and a large portion of the Democrats in Congress being opposed to the [Cleveland] administration on that question, opportunities were afforded for mixing politics. The old places where the little band [of Populists] formerly met for conference were never again so used. With the advent of the silver question, the leading ideas in the Populist creed were obscured by the silver glare, and they were allowed to drop out of sight.

When questions of floor management, distribution of patronage, appointment of committees, or other parliamentary details were pending, Populists met, as the other parties did, and determined their line of policy. But in no instance was such a meeting held to agree upon and formulate a bill or resolution to be introduced as a measure embodying distinctively Populist doctrine on any subject, though that policy was often urged in the beginning. An examination of the *Congressional Record* shows that bills on the same subject were introduced at random by individual members, and in most instances were never heard of afterwards. And as to the most vital contentions of Populists in the ranks, they received less attention from Senators and Representatives than minor and less important matters.

That part of the money question which is most essentially and distinctively Populistic was embodied in bills in the House by Davis and Otis of Kansas and Howard of Alabama, and in the Senate by

Mr. Peffer. These bills provided for government loans, in certain cases, on land as security. Howard's bill provided for a subtreasury scheme on the plan of the Farmers' Alliance, and Peffer's bill coupled this feature with his plan to establish a bureau of loans. This part of the Populist creed was never pressed in Congress by any other persons than these here named.

Another vital tenet of the Populist faith is the referendum, for which Howard and Skinner in the House and Peffer in the Senate contended alone.

These two subjects—government loans and referendum—never have been taken up and pushed by Populists as a body in Congress. Populism has run to silver and is dying in the arms of Democracy from political anemia.

Demo-Populism has divided the party beyond hope of reconciliation. That was evident from the proceedings at the [1897] Nashville and [1898] Cincinnati conventions, and recent investigations show that the party is not only divided, but many of the old members are going back quietly into the organizations from which they came. The *New York Sun* has directed personal reports from its correspondents in the Populist States of the West and Southwest during the time that some of these articles were being written, and the reports confirm and emphasize the showing made by official election returns quoted herein. Arrangements are already made or are being made in all the fusion States for a combination of some sort with one or [the] other of the old parties next year. The fusionists enjoy the advantage of having the party machinery in their own hands, and they retain the party name. They can trade and make such alliances as they choose for 1900 and await the outcome.

The spirit and the courage of the middle-of-the-road people is worthy of all praise. They have not been and they will not be seduced by the Democracy. In the Northern and Northwestern States, where they are greatly in the minority, and especially where the Australian ballot law is in force, they will have to unite with some other reform organization in order to get their candidates on the official ballot, or

THE AMUSING POLITICAL HAYSEED — His intellect is very
ordinary; but his whiskers are the wonder of the country.

*This 1895 cartoon confirms Peffer's own continuing commitment to
"wild ideas" and "Populist Dreams" (Puck, January 30, 1895). The
combination of Peffer's radicalism and such caricatures led Theodore
Roosevelt to describe him as "a well-meaning, pinheaded anarchistic
crank, of hirsute and slab-sided aspect." (Roosevelt to Brander Mat-*
thews, December 9, 1894, in Elting E. Morison, ed., The Letters of
Theodore Roosevelt *[Cambridge, Mass.: Harvard University Press,
1951], 1:411)*

else they will lose their votes.[1] This course already has been adopted in Ohio and is being considered in several other States.

In the Southern States, on account of local considerations, it may be found best eventually for these devoted men to make common cause with Republicans, as in other years they have done in Alabama, Georgia, North Carolina, and Texas. Whether well founded or not, the belief that white men in that region cannot afford to divide on what they call the race question is general, and it is too strong to be overcome by mere party attachment. Rather than support Democratic policies, methods, and candidates, Populists in several instances, as shown by figures quoted in these articles, and in large numbers, too, running high in thousands, have supported Republican candidates rather than risk unnecessary estrangement of all white men of other parties.

And this suggests an important consideration in cases where Populists feel it to be their duty to choose between the Democratic and the Republican party. Away down at the foundations on which these two great parties rest they are wholly unlike, and in respect to the matter of difference the Democratic party is alone on one side and the Populist party is on the same rack with the Republican party on the other side. That is to say: The line dividing the Democratic party from its great antagonist is the line between the political power of the State and the political power of the nation. The Republican party believes the national government may do anything anywhere within the boundaries of the union that will promote the general welfare, and Populists believe the same, but Democrats do not. Where Populists begin to differ with Democrats is right at the bottom—on the foundation stone—with respect to the powers of government, State as well as national, and the line of difference reaches out into the details of administration.

1. For the many problems that the Australian ballot law "reform" imposed upon Populists, see Peter H. Argersinger, " 'A Place on the Ballot': Fusion Politics and Antifusion Laws," *American Historical Review* 85 (April 1980): 287–306.

But Populists and Republicans do not differ at the foundation. They are agreed there. To illustrate: When the Treasury was empty and banks (State banks were all we had) suspended specie payments, and we had a great war on hand, the Republican party had no doubt about the power of the government to provide a money substitute in the way of a paper currency, making it legal tender. Democrats in Congress opposed the issue and circulation of greenbacks, and their opposition was put on constitutional grounds. They said Congress was not authorized to make anything but gold and silver coin a legal tender in payment of debts.

That is the doctrine of the Democratic party today. That party believes in gold and silver coin, and paper currency redeemable in coin. But it does not believe in government paper currency. State bank notes form the favorite currency of Democracy. The party in national convention recommends the repeal of the tax which prohibits "State bank issues." The Democratic party opposed the United States bank note system. It was in violation of the constitution, they said. And the party opposes the present national bank note issue on the same ground.

Republicans, when the country was in peril, issued notes, irredeemable notes, without hesitation, and nobody but Democrats objected. And no promise of redemption was made until the war was more than two years behind us, and no provision for redemption was made until we were nearly ten years beyond Appomattox, and redemption was not actually begun until four more years had passed.

It is from our experience with the greenback that the Populist got his idea of a permanent currency made of paper, behind which the government and people stand firm as the eternal hills.

It was from a study of the national banking system that the subtreasury plan of the Farmers' Alliance originated. Government bonds are personal property, just as cotton is, and they are neither more durable nor valuable than cotton. Owners of bonds deposited them in the Treasury and received 90 per cent of their face value in notes, which they were permitted to use in banking, the government and the people being protected against loss by the property on deposit, which property would not be delivered to anybody until the notes are surrendered. Why could not warehouse receipts for stored and insured cotton be used for local currency where money was scarce and cotton plenty?

It was not, however, until the silver agitation possessed the people that the subtreasury scheme was fully developed. When Secretary Windom proposed in his silver bill to issue circulating notes against deposits of silver, Dr. Macune and his farmer friends cried, "Eureka!" They proposed to use cotton, grain, and tobacco, just as Mr. Windom proposed to use silver. The Windom bill did not pass, but the [Sherman Silver Purchase] act of July 14, 1890, was the result of discussions originating in differences of opinion about the merits of that bill.

Populists do not favor our national banking system, not because bill holders are not always safe and current all over the country, nor because it costs any more to borrow the bank bills than to borrow greenbacks or gold or silver coin, but chiefly because the national banking system is in practice a dangerous monopoly. Populists are not opposed to private banking, but they believe the power to issue circulating notes ought to be exercised only by the general government. Let bankers deal in private paper and exchange money and bills—do nothing but banking. Issuing notes to be used as money is not properly a part of banking. It is a governmental function, and ought not to be delegated to private agencies of any kind.

Our national banking system had a peculiar origin. Up to the beginning of our great war we had always had State banks and none other, except the United States Bank, which was a sort of fiscal adjunct of the government. The first one lived from 1791 to 1811, the second from 1816 to 1836. But State banks we had continuously from 1781 to 1861. Suspension of specie payments by the banks at the close of the year 1861, when money was much needed, made it obligatory on the part of Congress to provide currency for use by the government, as well as by the people. State banks with no specie behind them could not be thought of; and they would not serve present requirements anyhow, because they were local and their notes, even when they were backed by specie, were subject to discount away from home. Government business had been greatly enlarged of late, its transactions had been necessarily many times multiplied, and they were fast accumulating in all parts of the country. There was no time to stop and look through bank note detectors to find the standing of banks and the market value of their notes. Business was rapidly growing and the tide was rushing. What was needed and what must be provided was a national currency, one that could be used in any part of the country where the government credit was par.

But we always had been taught that redemption of circulating notes was a necessary condition attaching to any kind of bank notes, and as the government had no specie except what was coming in from the receipts of customs duties, and that was set apart for payment of interest on the public debt, it was necessary that the government put itself behind the national bank notes; and in order to avoid the incurring of any unnecessary obligations it was provided that the banknotes should be secured by the deposit of government obligations already issued. Then, if the government survived and was able to pay its debts, these notes would be paid before the deposited bonds were delivered to the owners. These essential features are incorporated in the title of the original national bank act as follows: "An act to provide a national currency, secured by a pledge of United States bonds, and to provide for the circulation and redemption thereof."

As before stated, Populists do not favor the national banking system, but they all recognize its great superiority over the State bank system advocated by the Democratic party. Were it determined that one or the other of these two systems is to be retained as a permanent feature in our financial policy, and were a choice between the two submitted to a referendum vote of the Populists, the returns would show that the State banks had received no votes.

The truth is that the Populist idea of a national currency issued by the government only, and paid out (distributed) through public

THE GRANGERS' DREAM OF CHEAP MONEY.

"The Grangers' Dream of Cheap Money" ridicules what Peffer describes in his memoir as *"the Populist idea of a national currency."* Reflecting the orthodox views of conservative Democrats, it portrays the federal Treasury as a windmill propelled by Peffer pouring out inflationary greenbacks for poor farmers. (Puck, July 8, 1891)

agencies, is based on the greenback and the national bank note idea. Substitute the greenback for all kinds of bank notes, then change the national banks into government institutions, reduce interest charges to actual cost of preparing and handling the money, and we have the Populist's monetary theory reduced to practice; and there is nothing like it or like the system out of which it has been evolved to be found anywhere in Democratic doctrines, antique or recent.

The greenback, the Treasury note, the legal tender paper money idea, the providing of a national currency, and the destruction of State bank issues and the establishment of national banks issuing circulating notes secured by the government, are all of Republican origin. Democracy had no part nor lot in originating any of them. And yet the fusion Populist proposes to ally himself with a party that originates nothing but opposition. Whenever we go down to the foundation of federal power Republicans and Populists are agreed; the beginning of their differences is seen when we reach details of legislative action.

This is, it would seem, a proper occasion for the writer of these articles to restate in this public manner what he stated privately to personal friends, nine years ago—that if Senator Ingalls had felt it consistent with his views of things to answer the questions submitted to him by the editor of the *Kansas Farmer* in February, 1890, and had he answered them as the editor hoped he would in view of his well known and frequently expressed opinions on the subjects involved in the questions, he would have placed himself in harmony with the Farmers' Alliance without in the least departing from the record of his party in the State or from his own excellent record as a Senator, and he would have received the hearty support of that paper in his candidacy for the Senate.[2] The

2. This statement is scarcely persuasive. In 1890 Peffer had repeatedly condemned the conservative Ingalls, who supported little of the Farmers'

editor of the *Kansas Farmer* was a personal and political friend of Senator Ingalls, and nothing would have pleased him better than a consciousness of having been instrumental in getting that gifted man at the head of a movement with which the paper was so intimately identified. Every person connected with the paper, from the President of the company to the janitor, was a Republican, and there was nothing in the creed of Kansas Republicans antagonistic to Alliance doctrines. A large majority of Alliance men were Republicans. As has been shown in these articles, about 48,000 of them then belonged to that party, and the recorded declarations of the party on silver, banks, and currency were in perfect accord with the demands of the Alliance.

In 1878, when Kansas had only three Congressmen, at each of the three district nominating conventions and at the State convention as well, the Republicans of the State officially declared themselves as favoring the substitution of greenbacks in place of national bank notes on the ground that the former were the better kind of currency. Here is a copy of the resolution adopted unanimously by the State convention:

> That experience has shown the greenback currency (the creation of the Republican party and under whose fostering care it has been brought to a par with coin) to be admirably adapted to the wants of trade, and to the end that there may be but one class of paper currency, we favor the withdrawal of the national bank notes, substituting therefor greenback currency, issued directly by the government, as the sole paper

Alliance program beyond free silver and explicitly rejected its central contention that government action could and should relieve agricultural depression. If Peffer had privately made this statement in 1890, he had done so to justify his reluctant decision to leave the Republican party. That decision, however, was not based upon the personal attitudes of Ingalls but upon the party positions adopted by the increasingly unresponsive Republicans and upon the popular expectations of the farmers' movement, which, by 1890, Peffer was riding more than guiding.

currency of the country. And we demand that it be issued in sufficient volume to meet fully the wants of business without depreciating its value; and that it shall be received in payment of all dues, public and private, except as otherwise specified by contract; that we are in favor of an honest greenback that shall always be worth its face in coin, to which end we favor a law of Congress by which the volume of greenback currency in circulation shall obey the natural law of supply and demand.

That resolution was adopted by Kansas Republicans in State convention at Topeka, the capital, on August 29, 1878. On the 15th day of the last preceding February Mr. Ingalls had delivered a powerful speech favoring certain phases of monetary reform, especially in the direction of an increase in the circulating medium through the restoration of silver coinage.

In 1890, during the period of great political excitement in Kansas, and when Mr. Ingalls' [reelection] case was pending, a free silver coinage amendment then before Congress was favored by ninety-nine of every 100 voters of all parties in Kansas. As late as January 14, 1891, just fourteen days before the election of Mr. Ingalls' successor took place, he delivered a speech in the Senate, from which two brief extracts will show how easily the Senator might have satisfied his friends in the Alliance movement eleven months before. He said: "There is, Mr. President, a deep seated conviction among the people, which I fully share, that the demonetization of silver in 1873 was one element of a great conspiracy to deliver the fiscal system of this country over to those by whom it has, in my opinion, finally been captured." And again: "Mr. President, there is not a State west of the Allegheny Mountains and south of the Potomac and Ohio Rivers that is not in favor of the free coinage of silver. There is not a State in which, if that proposition were to be submitted to a popular vote, it would not be adopted by an overwhelming majority." And in this speech of 1891 the Senator quoted a striking passage from his remarks in 1878, before referred to.[3] In view of all these facts and circumstances it is not difficult to conjecture the anxiety of Mr. Ingalls' friends in the Alliance up to the pivotal period in 1890, when it was determined to go ahead blindly, and without the powerful impetus his leadership would have given us.

It is predicted that the trust question is to be in issue next year, 1900. Mr. Bryan has announced as much, and he has declared war against these commercial mastodons, and he does it in the name and by the authority of the Democratic party. Fusion Populists, or Demo-Populists, as Mr. Simpson calls them, think they must remain under the wing of Democracy in order to be in an anti-trust party. Here again these deluded people are wrong.

The Democratic party is no more competent to handle this subject than it was to meet the slaveholders' rebellion in 1860–61. The constitution was in their way then, and that troublesome document will impede their progress now. It is only five years since a bill introduced in the United States Senate by the Populist Senator from Kansas to prohibit dealing in options and futures was opposed and defeated by Democratic Senators on the ground that it interfered with the rights and jurisdiction of States. And when the sugar trust demanded that one-eighth of one cent a pound duty on refined sugar should be written in the Wilson tariff bill it was put in, and every Democrat in Congress, except Senator Hill, voted for it, as did every Populist, save one.[4]

3. Again, Peffer is not convincing in this attempt to rehabilitate Ingalls and the Republicans of Kansas. At the time, Peffer had denounced this infamous "last chance" speech of Ingalls on January 14, 1891, as "conceived in sin and brought forth in iniquity." See *Kansas Farmer*, January 21, 1891. Moreover, after 1878 Kansas Republicans never again supported the type of monetary reforms called for in the section of that year's platform quoted by Peffer above.

4. Peffer's objectives are at cross purposes here, and the issues involved

The Democratic party is not constructed for work of this kind. During the long debates in Congress on the tariff bill in 1894, when both branches of Congress were Democratic, with all the important committees organized on party lines, and the President of the United States the most distinguished Democrat then on earth, and when the party could have passed any party measure that it desired to become law, and when Democratic Senators and Representatives denounced Republican tariff legislation as being the womb from which trusts issued, not one of them proposed to interfere with any of the more than 100 trusts enumerated in an impassioned speech by Senator Vest of Missouri, a Democrat of long and good standing.

Mr. Bryan and every other well-informed Democrat knows that so far as platform declarations against trusts are concerned, Republicans, having begun in 1888, have four years the lead; and that so far as legislation is concerned the only anti-trust law ever enacted by Congress was introduced, passed, approved, and put in force two years before the Democratic party ever so much as declared against trusts. On July 2, 1890, "An act to protect trade and commerce against unlawful restraints and monopolies" was approved by President Harrison. The bill was introduced by Senator John Sherman on December 4, 1889, and, being the first bill introduced in the Senate at that session, it was marked "Senate bill No. 1, Fifty-first Congress, first session." Following are two sections of the bill as it was passed and approved:

in the congressional voting on the Wilson tariff bill do not lend themselves to the simple analysis he presents. He wants to portray the Democrats in Congress as not being opposed to trusts in their votes on the bill, but their votes were in favor of limited tariff reform and an income tax, as were those of the Populists who supported the measure. Hill's opposition stemmed solely from his hostility to the income tax provision; Peffer's to the lack of a *graduated* income tax as well as the sugar duty. Peffer's understandable desire in 1899 to indicate the uncompromisingly Populist nature of his own voting behavior ironically undermines his attempt to show a discontinuity between Populists and Democrats.

Section 1. Every contract, combination in the form of trust or otherwise, or conspiracy in restraint of trade or commerce among the several States, or with foreign nations, is hereby declared to be illegal.

Then follow the penalties.

Section 2. Every person who shall monopolize, or attempt to monopolize, or combine, or conspire with any other person or persons to monopolize any part of the trade or commerce among the several States, or with foreign nations, shall be deemed guilty of a misdemeanor, and on conviction thereof shall be punished by fine not exceeding $5,000, or by imprisonment not exceeding one year, or by both said punishments, in the discretion of the court.

That law has been held good by the Supreme Court of the United States, and the Joint Traffic Association—a combination among railroads—was dissolved under its provisions. Whether it is broad enough to cover manufacturing trusts has not yet been determined, and if Democratic theories on State rights, as approved by the national party platform of 1896, are to govern, Congress will never be able to suppress any combination of persons not engaged in the business of transportation. The theory of that party is that manufacturing is a State matter, to be dealt with only by State Legislatures. If that theory is correct, then the trust question cannot be made an issue in national politics, except so far as it relates to transportation, and that has already been disposed of in the judicial determination above referred to.[5]

5. For an elaboration of Peffer's views on trusts and the role of an active government, including his position that "the right of the public to regulate all functions and franchises intended to serve the people is inherent," see his two essays, "The Trust Problem and Its Solution," *Forum* 27 (July 1899): 523–533 (quotation on p. 530), and "The Trust in Politics," *North American Review* 170 (February 1900): 244–252.

That party is slow going—always behind. It never sees a wrong until it is pointed [out] by another party, and never recognizes an opportunity until it is passed. It has been of no use to the country during any period in the last forty years, and there is nothing in its creed or its history to attract any Populist who believes in the doctrines of his own party.

Democracy is behind Republicanism in everything. Conditions have so changed in the last few years that the coinage question has practically dropped out of politics. Nobody cares to hear about 16 to 1 now. The coinage issue was raised because it was thought there was not money enough in the country, but the increase in the world's production of gold has been great enough to fill the void occasioned by the loss of silver coin complained of. For the year 1860 the gold output of the world was reported to be $134,083,000. That amount was not again reached until thirty-two years afterwards. There was a steady decline during twenty-five years. This aroused much anxiety about the future of the precious metals, and the silver excitement was the result.

But there has been an unprecedented increase of late years— enough, it appears, to fully compensate for the loss of silver. From 1890 the world's production of gold has been as follows:

1890	$118,848,700
1891	130,650,000
1892	146,651,500
1893	157,494,800
1894	181,175,600
1895	199,304,100
1896	202,956,000
1897	237,504,800

In eight years, beginning with 1890, the production has doubled. It is estimated that the figures for 1898, when collected, will foot up at least $285,000,000, and for the present year, 1899, they will exceed $300,000,000.[6] The south African gold fields are wonderfully productive. They are now mining gold at a depth of 5,000 feet, and getting $10 to $15 out of a ton of rock, within a day's walk of Johannesburg. Gains are reported from Australasia, Africa, Mexico, Alaska, and the United States. Colorado is now turning out nearly as much gold as the whole country produced a few years ago.

As long as there is an abundance of gold to supply the demand for metallic money in large transactions, the silver question will not be big enough to make a campaign on. The people never worry about anything they have no use for. And take 16 to 1 off the program, what is there left with the Democrat party that Populists ever had any sympathy with?

Another important fact in this connection is the rise in prices since 1896, instead of a decline, as was anticipated and predicted. Mr. Wharton Barker, editor of the *American* of Philadelphia, and candidate of the Middle-of-the-Road Populists for President in 1900, a careful statistician, has been keeping track of prices in general since 1891, and twice a year he publishes his tables showing the rise and fall of prices during the last preceding six months and for the whole period since '91. In the *American* for May 6, 1899, is a table carrying the calculations to April 1 of the present year. Explaining the table the editor says: "The summary of index numbers which we append shows that the general purchasing power of $88.78 on April 1 last was as great as the purchasing power of $100 on January 1, 1891, and a glance at the last column in the table, or the general index numbers, will show that prices taken in the aggregate are higher today than they have been at any time since October 1, 1893."

Of course, we do not know how long prices will keep up, nor can anybody foresee what will happen in that direction in [the] future,

6. For corroboration of the figures in the table and Peffer's estimates for 1898 and 1899, see John D. Hicks, *The Populist Revolt: A History of the Farmers' Alliance and the People's Party* (Minneapolis: University of Minnesota Press, 1931), 389.

because there are many uncertain factors affecting prices. But we all recognize as true that prices are better now than they were in '96, that people are more generally employed, that wages are better, business is better, times are better, money is more plentiful and can be borrowed on better terms.

Why, then, dear brother Populist, not recognize these facts, drop back into more congenial companionship, and get away from the blighting influences of the Democratic party. That party ought never again to be intrusted with national power. No party ought to succeed under a free government when "one of the main foundations of its political creed" is a standing menace to the peace of the people and permanency of their rule. That party's original State rights doctrine, as affirmed in '52, '56, and '60, was reaffirmed in '96.[7]

A party that is too blind to recognize its blunders cannot be trusted to distinguish between right and wrong, even when the light is turned on both of them.

A party too old to comprehend the changes of a hundred years is too old to handle the problems of today.

A party that has outlived its usefulness, as the Democratic party did long ago, ought to ask the prayers of its friends and quietly get out of the way.

7. Peffer here apparently refers to the statements in the 1896 Democratic platform condemning "the centralization of governmental power" and endorsing "the maintenance of the rights of the States and . . . the necessity of confining the general government to the exercise of the powers granted by the Constitution." See Kirk H. Porter, *National Party Platforms* (New York: Macmillan, 1924), 181–182.

Index